Dear Barry,

I hope you
enjoy !

Successful

Leadership

All the Best,

Len

June 23, 2018

A Pragmatic Guide for Leading

Balanced Leadership

Leonard W. Heflich

BALANCED LEADERSHIP
A PRAGMATIC GUIDE FOR LEADING

iUniverse books may be ordered through booksellers or by contacting:

iUniverse
1663 Liberty Drive
Bloomington, IN 47403
www.iuniverse.com
1-800-Authors (1-800-288-4677)

ISBN: 978-1-5320-4425-0 (sc)
ISBN: 978-1-5320-4427-4 (hc)
ISBN: 978-1-5320-4426-7 (e)

Library of Congress Control Number: 2018903909

Print information available on the last page.

iUniverse rev. date: 06/08/2018

Preface

Leadership is complex, nonlinear, and messy for the simple reason that people's behavior is complex, nonlinear, and messy. Leadership can be fascinating, frustrating, rewarding, and often untenable. A prescriptive or definitive model for effective leadership does not exist—and there have been many attempts over the past several thousand years! The root cause behind failed businesses and failed governments is usually either a lack of leadership or the presence of destructive or ineffective leadership. Leadership is critical to the success of any group of people. Groups need leadership. Are you ready and able to provide the leadership that your groups need?

I have traveled to manufacturing facilities in many different countries, which has afforded me the opportunity to observe differences in performance, style, and efficiency. These observations caused me to wonder, *What are the differences between the plants that perform well and the plants that need serious improvement?* Of course, there are many basic differences in culture, language, the neighborhoods, the buildings, the equipment, the people—even the weather! However, are these factors causative or merely contributing to the differences in performance? Could these factors be hiding the real cause of the poor performance or even providing excuses for inaction? Asking balanced, critical questions helped me to identify the root cause so that I could give the team concrete suggestions for how to improve. My conclusion, after many such assessments, is that the single defining difference between these facilities is the lack of effective leadership. When the leader is able to create a vision and build a capable team, magic happens, even in facilities that have failed for decades and even with the very same people who have gotten accustomed to failing for decades. The team gets engaged and excited. They find ways to overcome the obstacles that have, for years, been stopping them from performing better. If we are going to change our poorly performing facilities into great ones, we need to develop the leadership skills of our people. This book contains what I have learned about leadership, often the hard way. I offer these lessons to you in the hope that doing so will help you on your journey to becoming a better leader.

This book is not meant to be comprehensive or definitive. You will find here a collection of short dissertations on topics that are critical for and relevant to effective leadership. My intent is to be thought-provoking while not attempting to be the final word on any subject. We will consider leadership from a practical vantage point, with a focus on results. Balance is a singular but critical lens through which to view leadership. It will show you how best to lead a team to accomplish a challenge. You will learn how to make better decisions, build better teams, communicate better, be appropriately flexible, and be appropriately strong, thereby becoming an effective leader.

We will study balance in the decision-making process and consider how to select the proper balance in various situations, based on many factors. Balance is critical whether you are leading yourself or a team, facing a challenge, communicating, or making decisions. Each situation requires you to strike a balance of many factors. I do not claim that I have identified all the relevant factors—only those I have found to be most important.

Consider that each factor can be viewed as a continuum that goes from one extreme to the other. For example, when we speak of the strength of leadership, the continuum goes from very weak to very strong, with many gradations in between. The proper balance on this continuum may seem clear to you because of past experience or insightful thinking on your part, but there is usually no definitive black-or-white answer, just a gradation of gray in between the extremes. The objective in each case is to find the action, behavior, or decision that balances as best as possible the desired benefits with the inevitable costs. This point we will call the decision point. Your choices define your leadership and determine your success or failure. It is always possible to change your decision point; however, consistency is another attribute on which you must select a decision point. With too little consistency, you appear indecisive or weak. With too much consistency, you appear to be rigid, inflexible, or incapable of admitting a mistake. Balance does not imply compromise or a middle-of-the-road approach. Depending on the circumstances, which include you, your team, and the situation, the best decision point could be an extreme position on the continuum. Are you a tyrant, a wet noodle, or appropriately strong? Are you indecisive, immovable, or appropriately flexible? Do you talk too much, never talk, or communicate effectively? Do you see the importance of balance and the trade-off of cost with benefit involved in each decision? The trade-off is inescapable, and the balance that you choose is defining!

This book is dedicated to the memory of my Grandmother, Ann Becker.

She took me everywhere and instilled in me the value of working hard and having fun.

She taught me that there is no shame in being poor, only in being lazy.

Thank you Nan!

Acknowledgments

I have been fascinated by leadership for my entire career. Over the years, I have had many different kinds of bosses, peers, and subordinates who have helped me see the good and the bad sides of leadership, often forcing me to question my behavior, as well as understand theirs. It is this broad array of leadership styles and techniques that has helped me to see that there are no bad leadership styles, only effective and ineffective ones. It has helped me to see the importance of authenticity in leadership—that a style that works well for one person will likely work poorly for another. We are all individuals as leaders and as followers. There is no cookbook method for leadership. There is only balance.

I am fortunate to have had many mentors, supporters, and friends while researching and writing this book. I will attempt to mention them all, and I apologize for missing any. In roughly chronological order, they are as follows:

Berton Moore, Irwin Cooper, William H. Knightly, Dr. Charles Stewart, Michael Schwartz

James Kline, Leonard E. Burger Jr., Al Zwicker, Dr. Charles Manley, Dale Kuhn, Florence Weber Turk, Rodrigo Cunha, Michael Worth, John Phillips

Lee Sanders, Jeffrey Smyth, Theresa Cogswell, Rella Dwyer, Paul Stone, Joseph Maroun Jr., Gary Prince

Kevin Kraus, Andrew DeHont, Phillip Boehm Jr., Dr. Ross Ellis

Carolina Maria Brose

Mis amigos estimados: Vianet Galan Mendez, Stephy Simancas Bautista, Ismael Vega Garduño

My family: Lynda, Adrienne, and Brian Heflich

My mom: Marilyn

Thanks to all for your support and friendship.

Chapter 1

Balance in Leadership

The concept of balance permeates every facet of our lives as leaders and followers. There are trade-offs and consequences that we have to accept and deal with. Following are a few everyday examples of situations where the concept of balance is valuable. Consider the trade-offs and consequences that will result, depending on the decision point you select for each one:

- order versus disorder (What does your desk look like?)
- pain versus pleasure (It is often a choice!)
- force versus motion (Are you pushing hard and going nowhere?)
- up versus down (Is your head up or down?)
- hot versus cold (What is your mood today? How consistent is your mood?)
- increasing versus decreasing (Are you building or resisting change?)
- strength versus weakness (Are you strong or weak?)

- flexibility versus consistency (Are you flexible or consistent? You cannot be purely one or the other, and it's difficult to be both!)
- challenge versus routine (Are you challenging yourself and others or skating?)

But even balance must be considered in balance, meaning even balance can be overdone.

One of my favorite quotes follows:

> All things in moderation, especially moderation.
> —Ralph Waldo Emerson

As with moderation, too much balance can be a bad thing. We will talk more about this when we discuss the importance of being an authentic leader. We must be who we are—good, bad, and ugly. Moderation and balance are defining characteristics of our personalities, but so are our eccentricities and our wonderful, occasional lack of balance!

Being a leader inevitably involves making decisions, and every decision presents a dynamic balance between benefits and costs. For example, communicating in a clear manner is a good goal, but it can be overdone. Too much clarity or transparency in communication can offend or inappropriately divulge sensitive information. The leader must decide whether to err on the side of one benefit or the other, attempting but rarely finding the sweet spot that perfectly balances the benefits and costs inherent in each different situation. There is no free lunch; for every benefit, there is an offsetting cost. What is gained on one side is potentially lost on the other. The balance that you choose defines you as a person and as a leader. Balance is the essence of effective leadership and presents an inescapable dilemma in the act of leading.

Are you sure you want to be a leader? You cannot avoid that decision either! Not leading is a form of leading. If you are in a situation that requires leadership, then you must either lead or fail. Please don't get the idea that the situation is futile. There are good and bad consequences for any action we take, depending on the impact it has on other people. However, the outcome matters greatly, and we should not give up or give in. We must care deeply when considering and aiming for the proper balance and then be willing to accept the consequences, both good and bad.

Balance is yin and yang. It is feng shui. It is the sweet spot on a tennis racket or golf club. It is the story of *Goldilocks and the Three Bears*. It is getting something just right. However, since the world is always changing, the sweet spot is always changing too. What was in balance yesterday may not be today. Like riding a bicycle, we constantly need to monitor our positions and make adjustments to compensate for curves and bumps in the road. Balance is a difficult state to achieve and maintain, as it is a dynamic and constantly changing state. Unlike riding a bike, leadership has many elements. For each element, you must select the proper balance in order to be the leader you want to be. These elements are also highly integrated. The balance of each must therefore be consistent with the others in order for you to be a leader who is dynamic, reasonable, and dependable yet flexible enough to learn and change. Riding a bicycle is easy by comparison, as there are only a few elements to consider. Leadership is, in essence, riding a multidimensional bicycle!

Balanced leadership requires that we consider what is lurking on the other side of the coin in every situation and in every decision that we make. With every good, there is potentially a bad—and vice versa. With every action, there is a reaction. For every behavior, there is a consequence. Practice looking at the other side of the coin, and consider the price paid for each decision compared to the benefit derived. Was it an optimal decision? Were the benefits worth the cost? Was the consequence worth the effort? Did we get the balance just right? Or are we out of balance and missing the opportunity to perform at a higher level?

Now maybe you're thinking, *I'm not the boss, so I don't need to be a leader. Leadership is not for me.* That is simply not true. We are all leaders and followers at the same time. Do you work with other people? Do you need help or support from other people to get your work done? Do you coordinate or direct the efforts of other people? If you are responsible for getting something done with the help of other people, you are a leader. It's possible that you are not leading enough or effectively and that you have not yet achieved the optimal balance between followership and leadership to maximize your performance. There may be an opportunity for you to perform at a higher level if you intentionally and thoughtfully involve other people in helping you get those tasks done (i.e., being a leader). If you have a boss (and we all have at least one), then you are also a follower. You cannot avoid being a follower, just as you cannot avoid being a leader. And actually, you may find that improving your abilities as a leader allows you to be a better follower.

In the next few sections, we will consider balance in different components of leadership, including authenticity, vision, pushing versus leading, managing versus leading, ownership, strength, flexibility, polarity, planning, and execution and then how to put all the pieces together to become a great leader.

Authentic Leadership

Now here is a revelation: you are not a perfect leader! And you never will be. The best news is that you don't have to be a perfect leader to be a great leader. In fact, your flaws and idiosyncrasies are what make you human and interesting as a person and as a leader. Strive not to be perfect but rather to be authentic. Bill George introduced us to the concept of the authentic leader in his book *Authentic Leadership: Rediscovering the Secrets to Creating Lasting Value*.[1] If you haven't read it, do. It is an outstanding book on leadership. He talks about how being authentic to yourself and with others can make you a great leader in spite of—or actually because of—your flaws.

Trying to be something or someone you are not is a sure way to lose your balance in leadership. You may admire Rudy Giuliani as a leader and what he accomplished in leading New York City after 9/11, but you are not Rudy, and you never can be. You can learn a lot from him and even use some of his techniques, but you must assimilate those techniques as skills that are consistent with your personality and character. We will talk more about this in detail later. The point is that in order to strike a balance that is right and authentic for you, you have to be you.

> Be yourself; everyone else is already taken.
> —Oscar Wilde

Many people are not satisfied with themselves or their character. This in itself may not be bad, but taken too far, it can lead to insecurity. Once again, balance is important. If you don't like yourself, what makes you think anyone else will? We are who we are, and we need to embrace that person rather than trying to change ourselves. We need to accept ourselves and give ourselves some space to be different. It can be useful to listen to what other people think about our character and performance, but remember that we cannot change our character. We can change and improve our behavior and skills, and should always be working on doing so, but this is not the same as changing ourselves. We are still the same person, only more capable. More about this later too.

I once attended a training session on communication skills. The leader was Dr. Charles Stewart, who became one of my most influential mentors. Charlie started the meeting with a one-hour cocktail party to allow everyone to meet. There were only ten people in the class, so it was easy for us to meet each other. Now, of course, I knew that I was there to learn how to improve my communication skills, so I was on my best behavior during that cocktail hour! I was trying my best to be unauthentic and better than I actually was. After it was over, Charlie sat the group down and asked us to write a short description of the strengths and weaknesses of the people we had just met. I was amazed at how insightful and accurate their descriptions of me were, especially given that we had just met informally for one hour. We think we can hide our character flaws from others, but we cannot. We can run, but we cannot hide!

Being authentic is really just about being honest with yourself and others. Admit your flaws and shortcomings, laugh about them, and invite others to help you overcome them. People will respect you for your honesty. You build trust and strong, sharing relationships based on honesty. Cover up your flaws, and other people will see right through the camouflage and learn that they cannot trust you. If you cannot be honest about yourself, what other lies or half truths will you try to put over on people? Do you really think that people are blind and cannot see? Your lack of honesty and candor is an insult to other people's intelligence and a waste of everyone's time. Admit your flaws and weaknesses and ask others to help you with them, and they will.

Don't take yourself too seriously. You may be an important person, working on important projects, but having humility is valuable when you want to relate to other people in a positive and cooperative manner. We can accomplish little by ourselves. We need to build a strong and effective team around us to achieve anything. We will talk a lot about the value of humility and humor when we talk about servant leadership, teams, and motivation.

> Excuse me—it appears that you are unable to
> laugh at yourself, would you mind if I do?
> —anonymous

Leading with a Vision

Balanced leadership requires a vision that communicates what we want to achieve and why, so that people can understand and align with us and with each other. The most effective and powerful way to challenge an entire organization, a department, a team, or a person is to create and communicate a vision. A vision is a simple description of a desired future state that we want everyone in the organization to work toward. It is not a dream. It is a description of a real and feasible potential future state worthy of achievement by a person, team, organization, or company.

Accomplishing the vision will require lots of change and effort by many people, and in order to be successful, these changes and efforts must be coordinated and in balance. Balance does not imply stasis. People need to understand in order to unite and join together to achieve the vision by keeping their efforts in balance with the rest of the team. Great leaders lead people to accomplish goals that they would not have attempted or achieved on their own. They challenge people to attempt and achieve greater performance. How do they do this?

A vision statement must pass an elevator test in order to be effective and easy to communicate. If you cannot state it in the time it takes to ride an elevator, then it is too complicated to be an effective vision statement. Ruthlessly trim your vision statement until you can say it in less than ten seconds to anyone, without misunderstanding, so that you and your people can repeat it often. Some people say, "That's only a slogan." It is more than a slogan when everyone understands that the statement describes a relevant and meaningful future state. A good vision statement hits people in the heart. As the leader, you must communicate the vision in everything you say and, more importantly, in everything you do. You cannot overcommunicate a vision. It needs to permeate the organization to coordinate, align, and direct everyone's efforts. It is the most powerful way to do so.

Consider some powerful vision statements:

- John F. Kennedy: "We will put a man on the moon and return him safely before the end of the decade."
- Walmart: "Everyday low prices."
- Winston Churchill: "Victory will be ours," reinforced by the ubiquitous two-fingered V sign.
- Boy Scouts: "Be prepared."
- US Marine Corps: "Semper fidelis" (always faithful).
- Martin Luther King Jr.: "I have a dream."

Is there any question what these simple, powerful, emotional, and galvanizing statements mean to us and the people they lead? Martin Luther King appealed to the world with his simple statement in 1963, and still these words motivate people everywhere to work toward a desired future state. We are motivated by this statement to work in our own way, each person according to their ability and situation. We have not yet reached the desired state that these words describe, but we continue to strive, improve, and judge our current situation against the standard that these words create. Please note that MLK did not say, "I'd like to see all people living and working together in peace." This states the same basic sentiment of the "I have a dream" vision, but it does not convey the emotion or the visionary power. The statement "I have a dream" is emotionally charged; it can send shivers up and down our spines. We cannot argue with the powerful feelings embodied in this statement. We do not misunderstand the meaning of the words, even though they are simple and do not give us details about the desired future state or the steps necessary to get there. These powerful words do not need to go into detail, as we know and feel what they mean. This is a powerful and enduring vision statement. The other vision statements that I have listed as examples may not be as emotional or as personal, but they are still simple and effective statements of a desired state that drive the behavior of all the people led by them.

> A vision without a task is but a dream.
> A task without a vision is drudgery.
> A vision with a task is the hope of the world.
> —Donald Zimmerman

Involve your team in developing the vision. The discussion around what the vision should be and what it looks like is a great team-building exercise that will help align your team. A vision is not a dream. A vision is a description of some achievable and real future state that we all need to understand, embrace, and work on collaboratively to make real. It needs to be real and achievable.

> He who has a why to live for can bear almost any how.
> —Nietzsche

The vision is almost never to make money. This is a common mistake people make when designing their vision. Making money is a result of achieving our vision; it is never the vision itself. Why is this so? Making money is a critically important result of our activities and of achieving our vision. Money is an enabler that allows us to perform our activities, and our activities allow us to make money. It is a virtuous cycle. Nevertheless, the focus of our vision must be on the activities and not on the money. The money is a result, not the vision.

This point is important, so let's consider in some detail what we do and how we make money. In our business, we buy *stuff*, perform some *activities* on it, and then sell some *products* to our customers. This simple model works whether we make cars, toys, or food; sell a service; mow lawns; or are a bank. We bring in a raw material, perform some special activities, and deliver a product to a customer. This is our mission, the reason we exist as a company or organization. If all is well, we have added value to the *stuff* by our *activities*, and the customer is willing to pay us more for the *products* than it cost us for the *stuff* plus the *activities*. The difference between what the customer is willing to pay and what it cost us is our profit. Remember that our customer, if they wanted to, could buy the stuff and perform the activities themselves to produce the products, thereby saving themselves the profit that we take. Again, if all is well, they don't want to do this. They prefer to pay us for the products we produce because the activities we do are known only to us, or we are more efficient at it then they would be, or there are other reasons why they prefer us to do this work. The result is we make money and the customer gets a value-added product that they are willing to pay for. What does this have to do with our vision? In order for this all to be true, the activities we perform must be special. After all, if what we are doing is not special or unique, then our customers will eventually go to another supplier or bring the process inside and eliminate us. The activities are what make us special and what motivate our customers to pay us more for the products we make than it cost us to buy and produce them. If we focus on making money, we may lose our focus and attention on the activities. This would be like killing the golden goose. The goose is what matters! Our vision must be on the activities we perform and not on the money we make as a result of these activities. Our vision must be about how we will further develop the activities to protect and enhance our position as a producer. We need to protect and breed golden geese in order to make more gold, not squeeze or kill the goose in order to get more gold!

A small team of people who have worked together can be a beautiful thing to watch. They don't waste effort or time. They back each other up to assure the success of each member and of the team, and they take pride in their work and in their performance as a team. They may even develop their own language—words, acronyms, hand signals, even sounds that have meaning only to them. You have probably seen sports teams like this. A team like this has worked together and bonded into a strong and supportive group. We want our teams to look and function like this, except we don't have time to practice, and in our business, the "plays" are not as predictable, so practice may not be feasible anyway. We barely have time to get the job done, so how can we create a team that delivers the result without the practice? We do it by leading the team with a mission, vision, strategy, and goals.

Some of the benefits of having and communicating a good vision include the following:

- Each member of the team can align their personal goals with the group vision.
- Everyone knows what is expected of them individually.
- The team is able to function as a unit in working to achieve the vision.

An effective program includes a mission, vision, strategy, and goals. These fit together and form a cohesive image of who we are, what we do, what we plan to better, how we will achieve it, and what steps we will take to get there. The mission is what we do, why we exist. The vision describes where we want to be some time in the future. The strategy is how we are going to achieve the vision. The goals follow from the strategy and are the steps we are going to take to make it all happen. We will discuss this in more detail in a later section.

When everyone works toward achieving the vision, their efforts align and combine, resulting in great synergy. We can perform like the well-practiced sports team without the need for practice, because we are all doing what we are expected to do, and we are all pushing in the same direction. I know my job and can do it well, while my coworkers know their jobs and do them well also. The issue, then, is not a matter of practice or even that we need to do our jobs better but rather that the team performs in a coordinated manner to work together for the same goal. Our efforts don't impede or detract from the efforts of our coworkers, and the job gets done. A good vision will allow you to align your team and lead them to success.

I was in a plant in Argentina, and after our tour of the facility, I asked the plant manager a few questions. It was obvious from the tour that the performance of the people, even though good, was not great, and there was not a lot of excitement or drive in his people. They were doing their jobs in an effective manner, but they weren't fully engaged as individuals or working together as a cohesive team.

I asked him the following questions:

- What is your vision for the plant?
- What do you expect to achieve here in the next three years?
- What will be different in the plant in three years?
- How will you be different in three years?

He was unable to answer, because he had never thought about these questions. I made the following suggestions to him:

- Work with your team to develop a vision for what the plant will look like in three years.
- Work with each manager on the team to develop a vision for their functional area.
- What will their functional area and their job look like in three years?
- The vision for each functional area must align with the vision for the plant.
- Once you have these visions, communicate them to everyone in the plant—over and over again.
- Define the steps to make the visions real.
- Finally, execute those steps one by one.
- Make those steps part of your projects and objectives over the next three years.
- Make the vision real!

I could tell by the look in his eyes that he got the message and understood what I was telling him. If he does as we agreed, it will change him, his team, and the plant. I want to go back in three years to see what happens! We use vision to challenge and lead individuals. We lead them by helping them to develop a vision for themselves and their teams that is consistent with and builds upon the organization's vision. Using a vision is a powerful way to lead and challenge people.

While I cannot fast-forward three years to see what happens in this plant, I can tell you about another plant where the leadership accepted and accomplished a huge challenge. We have a small manufacturing plant in one of the poorest countries in Central America, and it was performing poorly. It is in a dangerous neighborhood, in an old building, and they have old equipment and a young, inexperienced team. The problem was that this plant exported to the US market and therefore was required to be certified. Everyone thought that it was impossible, but we put in a new plant manager and challenged him to achieve the certification within two years. They did it, so I had to go see for myself. The team was positively busting their buttons they were so proud. They did it with little investment, with the same old building, the same old equipment, and the same team that had been there before. Typically, when I walk through a plant, I can find several issues to be corrected, but in this plant, as hard as I searched, I couldn't find any issue. They were not perfect but had found a way to comply with requirements in every area of the plant. The key to their success became evident when our group walked into a small room where the ingredients were scaled for production. The room was tiny but clean and well organized, and every utensil and pot was labeled. In short, it was impeccable and in full compliance. I asked, "Who did this?" The operator who worked in the room immediately stated proudly, "I did it!" The plant manager and the other supervisors stood by quietly and nodded, with big, proud smiles. This is balanced leadership at its best.

> Where there is no vision, the people perish.
> —Tao Te Ching

This is a powerful statement, especially considering that it was written several millennia ago. It is a bit extreme but expresses the importance of having a vision. Without a vision, the members of a team don't know where they are expected to go or what they are expected to do. They literally don't know how to behave. They will likely do what they think is right, which may not be so bad. However, there will inevitably be differences of opinion with their fellow workers, who are also doing what they think is right. If they have different views of what is right, there will be conflicts, and they will have a difficult time working together to achieve a common goal. If they do not have a common vision, their efforts are likely to conflict and create anxiety. They need a vision to define where they are going as a team so that they can align their efforts. The hands of many make the work easy when the hands are going in the same direction. A vision can be effective in any size group, including large, complex, or rapidly changing organizations. In fact, in large, complex, and rapidly changing organizations, having a vision is the only way to effectively lead. Without a vision, the people may not perish, but they certainly will flounder.

Leadership versus "Pushership"

Leadership is the practice of getting out in front of people and showing them the desired direction. Leaders get their power from the people they lead. When people follow a leader, they do so voluntarily. The result is a group of people who are self-motivated to work separately but driving in the same direction in a complementary manner. Leadership will fail when the leader is inconsistent or unclear about the desired direction, or in other words, leadership fails when there is no leadership.

Pushership is the practice of getting behind people and pushing them in the desired direction. The pusher exhorts people to do what they tell them to do. People will respond to being pushed by doing what they are told to do. There is little or no self-motivation, as the motivation comes only from the pusher. The result is a group of people who do what they are told even if it is wrong and who often contribute no more than what they are pushed to do. The efforts are complementary only to the extent that the pusher has anticipated and coordinated their efforts. Pushership can work well in a small organization where the pusher is brilliant and truly involved in every aspect of the effort. Pushership will usually fail in large, complex, or rapidly changing organizations.

The optimal situation is when we are able to appropriately balance leading and pushing for the people and situation we have. Pushing is not all bad and is needed to some extent, but there needs to be a balance between leadership and pushership in any organization or work situation. Some factors to consider when striking the balance between pushership and leadership are as follows in table 1:

TABLE 1

Leadership is best when there is:	Pushership is best when there is:
• High complexity	• Low complexity
• Changing environment	• Stable environment
• Low certainty about how to do the job	• High certainty about how to do the job
• High certainty about the goal definition	• Low certainty about the goal definition
• Boss has low expertise and staff has high	• Boss has high expertise and staff has low
• Long timeline or low immediate urgency	• Short timeline or high immediate urgency
• Self-motivated individuals	• Individuals who want to be told what to do
• Higher levels of the organization	• Lower levels of the organization
• Need to develop skills in people	• Skill levels are adequate or possessed only by the leader

Striking the right balance depends on the task and the people involved. A boss can use leadership to galvanize the overall activities of the staff toward a large, complex goal while using pushership to push specific people on specific tasks to assure urgent completion of those tasks within the overall framework of the complex, self-motivated, vision-led tasks. Some people actually prefer to be told what to do and how to do it, so they don't have to take any responsibility for making decisions. In general, and it is not mere semantics, leaders pull, while bosses push.

Dwight Eisenhower kept a rope lying on his desk. When asked what it was for, he would respond, "It will go anywhere you pull it but nowhere that you attempt to push it." The same is true in leadership.

Using a combination of leadership and pushership in an organization keeps people on their toes. A little pushership can be used effectively to assure that urgent tasks get done, while a healthy dose of pullership frees up the organization to work flexibly and in a self-motivated fashion to reach the bigger group goal. Too much pushership creates an organization where everyone waits for the boss to tell them what to do, crippling self-motivation and making the organization totally dependent on the boss. In the short term, the results can be good if the boss knows what to do, is capable of working at the necessary level of intensity on a sustained basis, and can juggle all the necessary tasks and priorities. That is a lot of ifs! If the boss leaves the organization or takes a break or a vacation, results will falter in their absence, as the people are not able to self-direct their own activities. Bosses in this situation often burn themselves out. In the long run, pushership is destructive to the organization, and failure is often the eventual outcome. On the other hand, too little pushership creates an organization where everyone is self-directed and working in a coordinated fashion to get the job done. That sounds pretty good and is the result we want, but what happens when something goes wrong, perhaps outside of our control, and we need the team to react immediately and urgently? The leader may need to step in and essentially put the self-directed work on hold for a short time in order to push the team to change direction and get some urgent task done. If the leader does this in a positive manner, explaining the need and urgency, they can increase team cohesiveness and confidence. Then let everyone go back to their normal behavior once the temporary crisis is over. The point is that there is benefit to both pushing and pulling our teams in the proper balance.

The higher up in the organization that pushership is used as the primary method for driving performance, the more destructive it is. Especially at the upper levels of an organization, self-motivated, coordinated, proactive behavior is critical to success. At lower levels of the organization, a boss can use pushership to effectively multiply their own efforts by personally directing the efforts of their staff. The negative impact of pushership in a small organization can be overshadowed by the benefits derived from a driven, talented, benevolent dictator. This is much more difficult to do effectively in a large organization. It is also much more difficult to achieve success in this manner at higher levels in the organization, where the loss of self-initiative in upper management would be devastating.

Corporate positions often resort to pushership to get other parts of the organization into uniform compliance. Corporate policy is designed to create uniform behavior in order to assure compliance, and by definition, there cannot be much room for individual determination. The best approach is to involve the people who will be impacted by the policy in developing and implementing it. Provide transparency in the process, explain the reasons for the policy as well as the intended objectives, and seek feedback for continuous improvement. The biggest mistake is for corporate policy to be imposed by those who are out of touch with the issues in the field, either because they don't have the experience or their experience is obsolete.

Sometimes the threat of pushership is enough to get people motivated to action. One of my favorite billboards says in large white letters on a solid black background "Don't make me come down there!" signed "God." Now that is a serious threat of pushership!

A major side effect of pushership is that subordinates do not develop or grow. Their skill level is static, and their performance is highly dependent on the boss telling them what to do and how to do it. After some time, people in this situation begin to believe that this is the way work is supposed to be done. They expect to be told what to do and how to do it. They no longer take self-initiative to make decisions that they honestly believe belong to the boss only. In this manner, self-initiative and self-improvement are driven out of their behavior. People like this can poison a group for many years as they demand that newcomers behave in the same way to protect their uninvolved working style.

Bosses who engage in pushership as their primary method of driving performance often justify their behavior based on the results that they are able to achieve. They even come to believe that their people are incapable of performing at the required level without their guidance and control. This of course becomes self-fulfilling and can be convincing to both the boss and the staff. The boss becomes a dictator, and the staff become robots. This leads to a negative spiral, with the staff becoming progressively less capable of self-motivated change and improvement. The boss owns the ideas, the process, and the results. The people perform at the level that the boss expects or lower.

Bosses who engage in leadership as their primary method of driving performance can also justify their behavior based on the results that they are able to achieve. They start out believing that people are capable of performing at the required level and then support their people to prove it. This can become a virtuous cycle with improvements continuously building on previous improvements. The competency level of the staff improves because of their taking self-initiative, making decisions, making an occasional mistake and learning from it, identifying opportunities for improvement, and taking ownership of the result. The people own the ideas, the process, and the results. The people perform at the level that the leader expects or higher.

Leadership can be difficult, but pushership is really hard work. With pushership, the boss is instrumental to the performance of the staff. The boss cannot take a break, much less a vacation, or leave to attend to some other important situation. A pusher must watch their people every minute to make sure they are getting the job done. A few-minute gap in the attention span of the boss can result in people goofing off or deviating from the required behavior. Since the people don't develop their skills under a pusher, when a new task or some change in procedure is implemented, the boss must be there to show the people what to do and how to do it. If the boss misses some key input or output, the people are not likely to observe or appreciate the importance, and failure will occur.

Think about some of the most effective leaders you have known and consider how competent they were at doing the jobs their organizations needed to get done. Chances are these effective leaders were not able to do the jobs of their people. In situations like this, the people realize that if the job is going to get done, they have to do it themselves. The risk that their boss may resort to pushership and tell them what to do and how to do it is very low because the boss is not capable or does not have the time. The result is that the people find a way to get the job done and meet the goal set by the leader. A technically competent leader who is capable or, even worse, more capable than their staff can have a difficult time leading people because the people are expecting the boss to tell them what to do.

The leader must make it clear to their people that they will avoid meddling in their work at all costs. Later, we will talk about developing people in detail and make the observation that competency develops in a vacuum. This means that as long as the leader steps in to take charge whenever there is a problem, the operator who is responsible (at least technically) for the situation will step aside and allow the leader to take over. This has several consequences, mostly negative. Of course, the leader, if they are competent, will solve the problem quickly, and everything can proceed along successfully. Sounds good, but that is the only positive result. The operator didn't learn how to fix the problem, so the next time it occurs, they will once again rely on the leader to step in to fix it. If the leader is not available, the result will be failure or at least a loss. Secondly, the operator will not be motivated to learn how to solve the problem unless they are a special, self-motivated type of person. The balance in situations like this is for the leader to teach and coach their team to solve the problem on their own, not to solve it for them, and then make it clear by their actions that in the future the team will be responsible for solving it without the leader's help. I like to say, "Keep your fingers in, but your nose out!" We want our people to be competent in their jobs.

Often, when time is short, the temptation for the leader to resort to pushership is even greater. Time is money, and a competent leader can solve a problem more quickly than anyone on the team. The benefit, as we have discussed, is short term, with long-term negative consequences and costs. It takes a strong leader to take the short-term hit in order to realize the long-term benefit, but after doing this a few times, people get the message. *They expect me to learn how to do this myself, to own it and to take responsibility for the results.* That is an important message and critical learning for the team. This is the cost of developing and educating your team not only to learn their jobs but to take ownership of them. I love this quote from Peter Drucker: "If you think training is expensive, try ignorance."

The other side of the time-management coin (and I want to emphasize the need to *always* look at both sides of every issue—or more, depending on how many sides it has!) is how the deadline was set. Perhaps the time allowed to perform a task is too short to allow the team to take ownership and learn. After all, learning takes time. Part of the balance in getting the deadline right is to assess the skills and capabilities of the team and build in time for learning if they are not fully capable. If there truly is no time, due to constraints outside of our control, then we may have to put off the learning for another day. Acknowledging this can minimize the damage and get the job done efficiently. Involving the team in the assessment and getting them to identify the skill gaps and needs for learning up front can make it a powerful team-building exercise.

My favorite bosses were those who helped me grow. They challenged me to improve, allowed me to experiment and make mistakes, and then supported me when I needed it to be successful. They allowed me to make mistakes but didn't allow me to fail. They knew when to lead and when to push, when to help and when to get out of the way.

The next time you have a project, consider these questions:

- Will you push or lead or strike some effective balance between the two approaches?
- How will you know if you have achieved the proper balance for your group and project?
- How will you know if you have pushed too much?
- How will you know if you have led too much?

Leading versus Managing

Leading and managing differ in many ways but most dramatically in the scope and the impact of influence that is possible. Managing is necessary or appropriate for controlling systems, programs, events, and small numbers of people, or when close control is desired. For example, when the manager has the expertise and the subordinates on the team are followers with little expertise or discretionary behavior. Managers create objectives and plans designed to get the job done. Leading, on the other hand, is necessary or appropriate for coordinating the efforts of large organizations and large teams, or when self-directed teams are desired. Leading is the most effective way to develop and direct a team, especially in complex situations.

It has always struck me as peculiar that in business we almost always use words that emphasize the *management* function while almost never talking about *leadership*. We call the area "management," call people in charge "managers," and use "management by objectives." Even "CEO" (chief executive officer) drips of management, without a hint of leadership. I suggest that we have the balance wrong, meaning that management is a critical function of managers, but leadership and being a leader are fundamentally different and also critically important. The higher up in the organization we look, the more important the leadership skills are and the less important, in fact even detrimental to performance, the management skills are. Table 2 describes some of the ways that leading differs from managing. The purpose of this comparison is not to say that one is good or the other is bad. On the contrary, we need to both lead and manage, often at the same time, depending on the specific challenge we are facing, our team, available resources, constraints, timing, and us, all in proper balance, of course!

TABLE 2

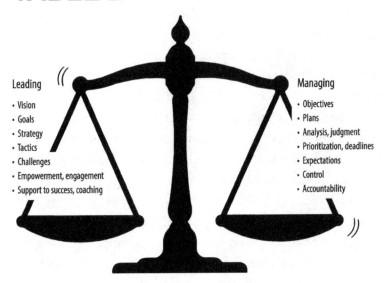

Leading
- Vision
- Goals
- Strategy
- Tactics
- Challenges
- Empowerment, engagement
- Support to success, coaching

Managing
- Objectives
- Plans
- Analysis, judgment
- Prioritization, deadlines
- Expectations
- Control
- Accountability

We need objectives to manage a project, while we need vision to lead a group of people in being self-motivated to work toward a goal. Managing is hands-on, often doing the work, where leading is sufficiently hands-off in order to get others to do the work. At its simplest, managing is doing where leading is getting others to do.

The concept of balance is critical when considering leading versus managing. These are rarely pure, mutually exclusive concepts. It is appropriate and necessary for us to manage and lead at the same time. We lead by creating a vision, strategy, tactics, and execution. At the same time, it is appropriate for us to manage the team to develop the objectives and expectations, analyze the results, set the deadlines, and hold each other accountable to achieve the numbers necessary to meet the vision. When the situation demands instant and urgent response, it is more appropriate for us to be on the managing side. When we are building for the long term, we need to lead more and manage less. We will almost always manage and lead at the same time in varying proportions, depending on the task.

- Have you considered where you are on the manage/lead continuum and assessed whether you have chosen the right balance for your situation?
- Are you managing too much and doing too much?
- Do you think that you are the only one who can do the work properly?
- Are you working too hard or not getting your work done on time?
- What would happen if an emergency required that you take tomorrow off?
- Have you developed a team that will get the work done in your absence?

If you manage too much and lead too little, you are likely doing too much of the work yourself, and you will fail or burn out or both. You must build a team that works together and supports each other. This is what leaders do. They build a team to do the work that they alone cannot do. Leaders develop their people so that when an opportunity arises, they are ready for the next step. Strong, supportive teams of competent individuals who work together to get the job done don't happen by accident or by chance. There must be a leader who takes the time to recognize the skills and weaknesses of their people and then develops and builds the team's skills, behaviors, attitudes, spirit, and desire to work together to achieve the vision. This takes time and persistence, both characteristics of vision.

I hope by this point you are realizing that leadership has many elements and that you must select the proper balance of each in order to be the leader you want to be. There are many elements to consider and decide about. However, these elements are also highly integrated, and the balance of each must therefore be consistent with the others in order for you to develop yourself as a leader who is dynamic, reasonable, predictable (dependable), and yet flexible enough to learn and change. To assess how well you have done, consider the performance of the team you have built. Here are a few questions to ask:

- Do your people know what you stand for as the leader (i.e., your mission, vision, and values)?
- Do they know what your goals are for the team?
- Do they follow you blindly without question, or is there healthy discussion of the issues with you and among the members of the team?
- Are your people comfortable approaching you with both good news and bad?
- Do your team members own their work and their results?
- If you walked up to one of them and asked, "Who owns this area, machine, or project?" would you get a blank stare or a confident answer?
- Do your people care about their work—enough to spend extra time learning about how to improve it, without being asked?
- Is your team getting the kind of performance and results you expect from them?
- Are they achieving or exceeding the vision and goals, or are they coasting?

The answers to these questions will tell you how well you have done as the leader and whether you are an effective leader or not.

Ownership

The purpose of ownership is to get people to accept responsibility for a job done well rather than waiting for the leader or management to direct their efforts. They take the initiative to pull together the resources and organize the team to get it done. This is effective leadership at its best. The team takes the initiative and ownership to deliver a needed result. It can be as simple as cleaning up an area or as complex as designing a system to perform some task.

As the leader, you must own and take responsibility for the performance of your team. If the group is successful, give them the credit. If the team is failing or has issues, you must take responsibility. Do so visibly so that all members see you saying clearly and simply, "I am responsible for this failure; we have analyzed the situation, and we are taking actions to improve our performance." The use of "I" and "we" are not accidental or meaningless. If your team sees you taking the heat and supporting them to success, they will work twice as hard to be successful. Taking ownership of the failure is the most effective way to rally your team and make it clear to all that you are the leader. If, on the other hand, you take the position that you are either not responsible or that you "did your job," the team will abandon you and find a way to prove that you are at fault. Avoiding ownership for the failure will tell the team and others that you are not the leader, and they will not follow you. Take the heat for the failure, frankly assess what went wrong and what needs to be done to fix it, and then make it happen. Rally your team to success by setting the vision, goals, and action steps that need to be taken in order to be successful. Then support your people to success and give them the credit.

The concept of the leader as a servant to the group is an extreme way to describe the ownership that the leader must take. Read the excellent and now classic book *Servant Leadership* by Robert K. Greenleaf,[2] or any of the excellent more recent releases on the subject.

Volunteerism is an extreme form of ownership, where the team initiates and owns the entire process from vision to tactics. One observation I've made as I've traveled to other countries is that the concept of personal initiative or volunteerism is lacking. In the US, we almost take it for granted that if there is something wrong in our community, some caring citizen will organize a group of volunteers to address it. There are volunteers who own and clean sections of the local highways. These groups are recognized with a sign that says they maintain this section of the roadway. The Statue of Liberty needed to be restored before the bicentennial celebration, and the government didn't have the money to do it. A local group asked Lee Iacocca to organize and lead a team of volunteers to raise the money from donations and then get the work done in time. We don't wait for government to do it for us; we organize a group of volunteers, get the resources needed, and then get it done. This is not so common around the world. It is also not so common in companies, but the concept is the same. Volunteerism is an advanced form of ownership. If your teams are practicing volunteerism, it is an indication of a mature and effective team.

Strength

Let's consider in detail one critical attribute of a leader—strength. How strong a leader do you want to be? How strong do you need to be in order to be an effective leader? The decision point will depend greatly on you, on the people you are leading, and on the context of the situation that you mutually find yourselves in. We might think a good leader is a strong leader, and a weak leader is a poor leader. That would be overly simplistic and not correct in many situations. Let's examine the strength continuum and consider how to select our decision point.

At one end of the strength continuum, we have very strong,

and at the other end, we have very weak, with varying degrees of strength/weakness in between. We can further split strength into many attributes of what it means to be a strong leader—rigid, inflexible, demanding, solid, steadfast, definite, absolute, and micromanaging are a few that come easily to mind. You will find that it is difficult to describe the varying degrees of strength and weakness without using qualitative words that also imply goodness or badness. Don't allow the value that is implicit in the words to influence your selection of the decision point. It may be hard to think that micromanaging is a good behavior for a leader, but there are situations where in order to lead your team effectively, you may need to micromanage. Also, consider that your idea of a responsive leader is probably different from mine, making it even more difficult for us to agree on a definition of these terms. There is a continuum of behavior for each attribute that is relative to us and our team.

Table 3 below decomposes leadership strength into subattributes and describes each in terms of the two extreme behaviors and the midpoint in between. For example, rigid, soft, and responsive describe the extremes and the midpoint respectively on the continuum for the subattribute of responsiveness. A rigid leader is not responsive. A weak leader is soft and extremely responsive. The midpoint is a responsive leader. And so on for the other subattributes.

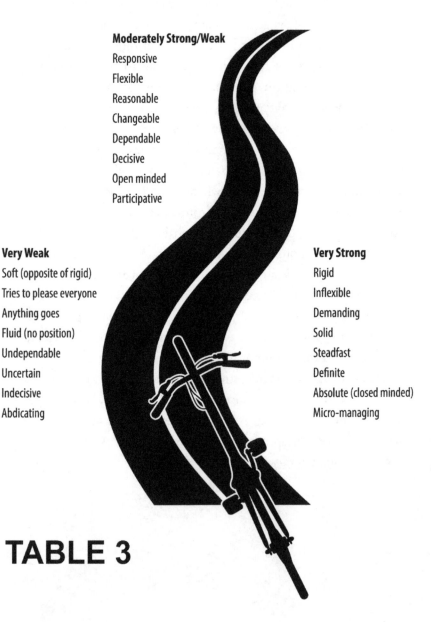

Moderately Strong/Weak
Responsive
Flexible
Reasonable
Changeable
Dependable
Decisive
Open minded
Participative

Very Weak
Soft (opposite of rigid)
Tries to please everyone
Anything goes
Fluid (no position)
Undependable
Uncertain
Indecisive
Abdicating

Very Strong
Rigid
Inflexible
Demanding
Solid
Steadfast
Definite
Absolute (closed minded)
Micro-managing

TABLE 3

Compare the attributes in the table above and consider the potential costs and benefits inherent in each behavior and the potential trade-offs. The costs are easiest to see at the extremes of the continuum. For example, the costs of being rigid or soft are fairly easy to see, while the cost of being responsive may not be so obvious. The benefits are easiest to see in the middle. For example, it is easy to see the benefits of being responsive and not so easy to see the benefits of being rigid or soft. But there are costs inherent in the moderate behavior and benefits at the extremes as well.

Consider Churchill and Gandhi. Churchill was an effective leader in wartime England under difficult circumstances that demanded strong and inflexible leadership. Once the war was over, England needed a different kind of leader, and Churchill was replaced by a more flexible leader. Gandhi, on the other hand, was a passive leader. He had tremendous resolve and commitment, so it would be unfair to say he was soft. But he was soft in approach and was able to lead the Indian people in a bloodless overthrow of English colonial rule. He was also replaced by a different style of leader after his tragic assassination. How effective do you think Gandhi's style of leadership would have been against Hitler? How effective would Churchill have been in leading India to their independence from England? I think the answer to both questions is "Not very!" Churchill exhibited the right leadership style for wartime England when they needed to stand up against Hitler. His style would not have been right for India in their fight for independence from England and probably would have started a war that India could not win. Gandhi's passive leadership style was exactly what India needed to galvanize a disparate population in a peaceful struggle with a military superpower that would have crushed an armed revolt. England did not know how to fight a passive war. Bullets and ships were not effective weapons against a passive, protesting populace. Choosing the right leadership style is critical to success and depends heavily on the situation, the goal, and the people being led.

I volunteered to fill the open position of plant manager in our largest and most complex manufacturing facility. Crazy, right? Actually, it was one of the most exciting challenges I have ever created for myself. The workforce was experienced and hardened, with some interesting characters in union leadership positions, selected mostly I suspect to be an annoyance to management. Past managers had attempted to manage the place and had failed rather miserably. The facility was labeled as unmanageable and too complex and was under consideration for replacement by several smaller facilities. I asked for permission to turn it around, and this became my vision statement. I made it no secret that we were failing and would be shut down if we didn't "Turn It Around." The changes needed were deep and painful, and to be successful would require, if not the support, at least the acquiescence of the workforce. Instead of being the strong "I will change you" approach that others had tried and failed with, I came in as a strong but flexible leader with the mission of involving the workforce in making changes in order to save their jobs. I made it a point of getting to know every person in the facility and talking to them as people as often as I could—daily if possible. My boss and I held around-the-clock meetings with the people to share details on business performance that had never been shared before in order to explain and get buy-in for the difficult changes that were needed. I explained that we would need to reduce the number of people in the plant as part of the changes. One man stood up and said, "Len, please tell us how many jobs will be cut. Don't nickel and dime me. Tell us the real number." I knew the number but hadn't planned on sharing it at that time. I considered the options but realized that this man and the workforce deserved an answer. And if I was going to be authentic and have any integrity with them, I had to give them the real answer. After some seconds of thought, I told them, "We need to cut one hundred jobs over the next three years." There was silence in the room, and the man said, "Thank you," and sat down. Several times, people came up to me to tell me how wrong it was to eliminate a specific job by combining positions. I asked if they would work with me and give the change a chance. The people always said, "I don't agree, but I'll give you a chance." I knew we had succeeded when, a few weeks later, the same person came back to tell me that they were surprised to find that it was working. We did go on to eliminate a hundred jobs in that plant over the next three years, and we did "Turn It Around."

If you are the leader of a group that is facing a survival challenge, such as bankruptcy, being rigid may be appropriate and necessary. A severe or urgent situation will generally require a more rigid approach. How does your expertise level compare relative to the group you are leading? If you are much more knowledgeable than they are, your best decision point will likely be toward the rigid end of the spectrum. If they are much more knowledgeable and experienced than you are, then you will probably be better off with a weaker, more responsive approach. Avoid thinking of weak as bad; it is a loaded word with a lot of baggage. Situations that require authority will drive the decision point toward rigid—for example, in the military or police. Perhaps your behavior is contingent on a contract or agreement that cannot be changed.

There are many benefits to the leader being strong. Your people will know where you stand and what you expect of them. They will be confident in making decisions in a predictable and unchanging environment. They will be more likely to deliver the expected results. They will not deviate from the specified goals and methods. Working for a strong leader can be exhilarating and rewarding. There are also some costs due to the leader being strong. If the leader is strong and the team is also strong, there is sure to be conflict. What if the leader is wrong? Very likely, the followers will follow the lead and fail, even when they have detected a flaw in the direction. If the leader is too strong, the followers may be unwilling to tell them that the plan is flawed. In these situations, working for a strong but flawed leader can be debilitating and demotivating. And even the most enlightened leader is wrong at least occasionally.

There are even possible benefits to the leader being weak. Your people will know that if the job is going to get done, they must do it. A capable team with a weak leader will step up to fill in the voids, in essence becoming self-led. They will deliver the results that they expect, which may be different, perhaps better than what the leader expects but may have failed to articulate. The team will work according to their own goals and methods, which could be very good. Working for a weak leader can also be exhilarating and rewarding, if the team is strong. If the team is weak, then there will be a lack of leadership, and the team will flounder and fail.

If you are leading a competent group in a dynamic situation requiring constant and immediate adjustments in behavior, due to changing conditions, then perhaps you cannot afford to be overly rigid or overly weak. In this situation, being responsive to the needs of your group may be the best decision point. If you are leading a group of expert professionals on a fun exercise, where the cost of failure is low, then perhaps you want to and can afford to be weak and allow your followers more freedom to experiment and learn.

Collegiate or collaborative situations call for weaker leadership. Weaker leadership does not imply the absence of leadership. It implies a leadership style that allows more independent decision making by the followers. If your followers are at the top of their game, you may want to be a weak leader that allows them wide latitude to do what they think is right. That is probably the best way to motivate them to great performance. The role of the leader in this case is not to dictate actions or even results but to lead the person or group of people to a goal or vision. Weak, responsive leadership of a group like this will often exceed the established goal set by the leader, perhaps by discovering something new that no one (especially the leader) could have predicted in advance. Is that effective leadership? Lao Tzu wrote in 600 BC, "When a great leader's work is done, the people say, 'We did it ourselves.'" That is a weak leader!

Perhaps you want to have self-directed work teams. Does this mean that management needs to be weak? Clearly, self-directed teams cannot work when management is micromanaging. It leaves the team no room to self-direct, and they will become frustrated and wait to be told what to do. On the other hand, self-directed teams don't do well when management abdicates their responsibilities and allows the teams to do whatever they want. The sweet spot is in the middle, where management participates in the decision-making process. The team is empowered to make decisions within guidelines set by management. Management participates in the process to the extent of keeping the team on track and assuring that the team is successful. This gives the team confidence that management supports their efforts.

Be careful when deciding how strong or weak your leadership needs to be in a given situation. Assess the cost/benefit trade-offs to find the right balance of strength and weakness for the situation and the people you are leading. Don't be afraid to be a strong or a weak leader; just make sure that you are effectively leading your group to the desired goal. Consider whether your approach is working and if it is right for the situation. If you are not getting the results you want, consider whether you are being too strong or too weak.

> He who, conscious of being strong, is content to
> be weak, shall be a paragon of all mankind.
> —Lao Tzu (600–550 BC)

Flexibility

Let's consider one of the subattributes of strength in detail—flexibility. By flexibility, I mean the ability to change when the situation requires it. A flexible leader listens to their team. They are willing and able to change in response to input. The extreme behaviors are being inflexible or trying to please everyone. Being inflexible means the leader will not change for almost any reason. They do not listen to reason. They are immovable. On the other extreme, a leader who changes behavior or tactics whenever anyone has a contrary opinion will flap around like a flag in the wind. In some extreme situation, that might be the best way to lead!

Flexibility can be a tricky behavior to balance. Whatever level of flexibility you choose, there will be some people who think you are inflexible and others who think you are giving away the store—at the same time. From a critical perspective, if you are giving me what I want, you are appropriately flexible. If you are not giving me what I want, you are inflexible. If you are giving others what they want and that is costing me somehow, then you are being overly flexible. It is a matter of difference of perception on your part and mine, and we are not likely to see it the same way.

From a constructive perspective, flexibility is the currency of compromise and reasonableness. If you bend a little and I bend a little, we can both get most of what we need and get along well. Flexibility is not a sign of weakness but rather a sign of resilient strength. The Chinese respect the bamboo plant for its ability to bend without breaking even under extreme stress.

Flexibility in leadership can encourage ownership. How would you feel if I came to you and said, "I need you to write a report for a meeting tomorrow morning. Get it to me before you leave today. I don't care how late you have to stay—make sure you get it done"? Contrast this approach with me saying, "I need your help pulling together a report for a meeting tomorrow morning that I just found out about. Tell me what parts you can handle, get some help from your peers, and tell me what you need from me. We must get it done tonight." The situation and the message are the same: I just found out about a report that is needed tomorrow morning, and we need to get it done before we leave the office tonight. The higher level of flexibility in the latter approach can convert this difficult situation into a positive team-building exercise instead of a morale destroyer. A little flexibility can grease the wheels of self-motivation and ownership. Note that the flexibility in this example is with regard to how the work gets done and who does it, not about the result. There is no flexibility in the expected result. So even in this simple example, there is a complex and dynamic balance of flexibility. Also, note that in the flexible approach, the boss offered to help. They did not take the ownership for getting the work done away from the subordinate. The subordinate is still in charge, and the boss has given them the power to direct them as needed. When you are the boss, offering to help in a situation like this will usually spur your people to get the job done without your help. If they cannot get it done without your help and they ask for it, jump in and help the team succeed. It will be a powerful team- and trust-building experience.

Excessive flexibility manifests itself in a perception of being untrustworthy, unreliable, wishy-washy, flip-flopping, and so on. A leader never wants to be seen as unreliable or untrustworthy. It's important to be choosy about when to be flexible and when not to be. Like the example above, we can be flexible about the how but inflexible about the what. As long as the result is delivered, perhaps we can afford to be flexible about the means by which it is achieved. There may be situations where time is extremely short or the result extremely critical, when we cannot allow any flexibility in the method or the result. The trick to balancing flexibility is in the degree of reasonableness that is possible in the given situation. If there is no opportunity to be reasonable, as in the case of the fixed deadline, then there is no opportunity to be flexible on that attribute. Is there a different attribute of the situation where reasonableness is possible and where we can be flexible? Be reasonable when you can and let the opportunity for reasonableness guide you in deciding where you can be flexible and where you cannot.

Polarity and Absolutes

The concept of balance implies polarity. Without the seesaw balance between the polar extremes, could there be an optimal balance point? The world is a polarized place where the presence of one pole enables the presence of the other. For example, there are polar opposites such as beauty and ugliness. Without ugliness, can beauty exist? Without pain, can there be pleasure? Likewise, there are good and bad, light and dark, hard and soft, north and south, hot and cold, and so on. What do polar opposites mean in the context of leadership? It means that, as leaders, we have to expect polarity in our people, our peers, our bosses, our business relationships. There are good and bad behaviors. Perhaps there are even good and bad people, but it is arguable whether anyone actually strives to be bad. There are strong people and weak people. We must not allow the presence of some bad in the people we deal with destroy our motivation or attitude, or even our desire to work with them or lead them. We must look for and encourage the good in people but not be so naïve as to think that there is no bad there too.

There are also absolutes and limits in the world that we must deal with. Stephen Hawkins asked, "What is north of the North Pole?" The answer is obvious but not trivial—nothing can be north of the North Pole. It is the absolute northernmost point. Likewise, in leadership. Some absolutes that we must acknowledge and deal with include zero, perfection, ignorance, arrogance, stupidity, integrity, and balance. What is more balanced than the balanced decision point? Can we have more integrity than absolute integrity? What is better than perfect? As leaders, we strive for the absolutes, recognizing that perfection, absolute integrity, and the optimal balance point are impossible to achieve and are fleeting due to dynamic change. Even if we could identify the perfect decision point, it will change in a minute, and once again we will be searching for the new optimum. The leader's work is a journey, not a destination. As soon as we get somewhere, we must start moving toward the next vision or goal. Once we achieve something, we cannot stop to enjoy it for very long. The enjoyment must come from the journey toward the goal, even if we never actually achieve it.

One place where polarity and absolutes can be useful is in communicating the vision. The best vision statements describe an aspirational, exciting, motivating, and even emotional extreme condition worth striving for, not a middle-of-the-road compromise situation. Remember MLK's "I have a dream"? It describes an extreme and emotional state that we must strive for and may never reach, although it is not impossible. It is easier to define and communicate the vision in polar or absolute terms, even if we agree that it will never be fully achieved. Balance does not imply compromise or middle. Sometimes the best balance is at the extreme!

Planning

Vince Lombardi is credited with saying, "Plan your work and work your plan." The more complex the work, the more important it is to have a well-thought-out plan and a contingency plan in case plan A runs into trouble. We cannot know in advance when a plan will fail or the situation will change, making the original plan obsolete or ineffective. Spending the time beforehand to consider what can go wrong and having a contingency plan ready makes it much easier to handle the problem when it arises. When considering what can go wrong, ask questions like "What is the worst that can happen?" and "In what ways can this plan fall short?" or "What can change that would impact our plan?" If the worst is not so bad, then don't worry about it—you can handle it. If the worst is really bad, you better have an alternate plan to mitigate the impact. Being prepared for the worst and planning for the best is good advice. As Ben Franklin said, "Failing to plan is planning to fail."

Prioritization can be an important part of planning, but it can also be a waste of time. It is a useful technique if you have a list of work to do and only the most important things on the list have to get done. If you absolutely have to get it all done, then what does prioritizing the tasks do for you? Perhaps you can work on the most important tasks first, but that is planning to allow the less important tasks to go last and maybe not get done. If that is failure, then your plan has failed. If you have to get it all done, put together a plan to get it all done and don't waste time planning for failure. Usually that plan will look different from a straight prioritization by importance. Since all the tasks are important, it really doesn't matter which one you do first and which is last, as long as they all get done. Focus on a plan that delivers the results, not a plan that delivers only part of the results.

Planning the future is a tenuous practice, best left to your vision. Knowing with any certainty where you want to be next week, next month, and next year is risky but also not to be ignored. Did I say balance? Leave the long-term planning to your personal mission and vision and put together a short-term plan of steps to achieve them. The best approach is to take your big long-term goals, break them up into little pieces, and then work now to get some of them done. Many people wander through life without a vision or a plan, bouncing from one opportunity to another, depending on what comes their way. How much more likely are we to get somewhere if we know what we want to do, know where we want to go, develop a plan to get there, and work at it every day?

"Would you tell me please, which way I ought to go from here?"
"That depends a good deal on where you want to get to," said the Cat.
"I don't much care where," said Alice.
"Then it doesn't matter which way you go," said the Cat.
"So long as I get somewhere," Alice added as an explanation.
"Oh, you're sure to do that," said the Cat, "if only you walk long enough."
—From Lewis Carroll's *Alice's Adventures in Wonderland*

We all eventually get somewhere after working long enough. Is that somewhere even close to where we wanted to be or what we are capable of? What are your strengths and weaknesses? What are you working on to improve? If we wait for a day when we have the time to work on improving, we never will. Find ways to fit improvement efforts into your daily routine and make it part of your plan.

I always wanted to be somebody, but now I
realize I should have been more specific.
—Lily Tomlin

I like to keep lists to remind me of what I need to do. I have several tiers of lists. I have a master list that is a comprehensive list of all the tasks I want to work on. I refer to this list every morning to refresh my memory and to ask, "What can I do today to move that task one step closer to completion?" I make a daily list of those tasks. It could be a very simple task that moves a complex project one step closer to completion. Maybe I can send an email to someone to get some necessary information. Maybe I can set up a meeting. Maybe I can do some research online. Maybe I need to go to a store to buy something. Whatever it is, as long as it moves the project along, it is a good task to do. This works for me because I can work on many different projects at once, moving each one along a step at a time until completion. It also keeps me from getting bored as I bounce from one task to another. The important thing is to get the work done.

> There are three kinds of people:
> People who make things happen
> People who watch things happen
> People who wonder what happened?
> —NASA astronaut James Lovell

Execution

Getting the job done is the bottom line. We are accountable for delivering results. Promises and good intentions don't count. Organizations that focus on and reward results are usually successful. The goal has to be doable and include a reasonable stretch to be meaningful and rewarding economically and psychologically. *Execution* is a great book by Larry Bossidy and Ram Charan.[3] It talks about the discipline of getting things done.

What does execution have to do with leadership or balance? Your leadership will be judged by what you and your team are able to accomplish. What have you done for me lately? The balance you choose for your decision points will determine the success or failure of your team to execute. You can build what appears to be the best team in the world, but if they don't get the job done, then it was for naught. How many times have you seen a baseball team packed with star players get beaten by a group of rookies? Or in football, the team marches down the field ninety-five yards and then fails to get the ball into the end zone. Failure to execute. After cutting away all the excuses, underneath you will find a failure to balance some attribute.

Here are some pointers on getting work done. First, break the work up into reasonable-size pieces and assign them to your team. Assure that everyone has the skills, tools, and time to get the job done and everyone is clear on what is expected and who is responsible. When a task gets done, take a second with the team to review it, acknowledging the good work and considering if the work has met the expectations. If yes, celebrate for a nanosecond (thanks, Gary Prince!) and move on to the next task. The brief review and recognition that a task has been successfully completed gives everyone a moment to recover before working on the next task that needs to get done. We get a feeling of accomplishment when we complete a task. Breaking the work up into small pieces means we will have a lot of opportunities to feel the accomplishment of achievement. This is a good thing! Never waste an opportunity to recognize a job well done, no matter how small.

Reward yourself and the team when the job is done. The rewards do not have to cost money. Recognition and a pat on the back are often the best rewards. When I work by myself, I think, *When I get this report finished, I'll have a cup of coffee.* That is enough of a reward to motivate me to stick to the task and get it done. The same technique can work well with a team. I was once the manager of a development group, and every few months, we had the additional task of preparing hundreds of perfect samples for a consumer test. We needed everyone on the team working together for a long day to get it done. This was in addition to our normal work, so motivating everyone was a challenge. We made a special event of it with the promise that as soon as we were done, we would go to a local restaurant where I was paying. The reward motivated the team to come in early and work hard to get the task done as quickly as possible, so we could go out and party. Not only did the work get done on time, but it was a great team-building experience. We had fun, and instead of it being a dreaded day of extra work, the team actually looked forward to these "special" events.

People will often say, "I will give it my best effort" or "I will try my best." I really hate when they say that! What will they do if their best is not good enough? Will they give up without further effort? And what does *try* mean? I'll succeed if things go well? I'll deliver the results if it is convenient for my schedule? Nonsense. There is no room for "your best" in execution. We have committed to get the job done, and if our best is not good enough, then we better find another way. Get help if necessary. If we have done our planning properly, we have already assessed the situation, identified the potential risks to the project, and developed contingency plans. Plan for success, not failure, and don't *try*—get it done, one way or another.

Don't accept failure! This sounds obvious, but we often design systems for failure. How many defects do you allow in your system? Likewise, don't allow members of your team to fail. This is what effective leaders and successful teams do—they support each other to success and don't allow anyone on the team to fail. I often visit a plant and see a step in the process that is producing waste. I stand there and watch the waste being generated. I ask the person I am with if they see what I see. They acknowledge the failure and agree that this is how this step in the process normally works. What can we do to fix it? It is not clear. Can it be fixed? Also, not clear. Okay. The role of the leader in this situation is to engage the right person on the team to find a solution and not to accept that "this is how it works." The leader can send a powerful message to the team by not accepting the failure. *This is not how we work. Let's find a solution and make sure it works.* Failure is a cancer that destroys team performance. When people get used to failing, it destroys their ownership. They ignore the failure and learn to accept it. Engage and challenge the team to eliminate the failure in order to deliver meaningful success and develop a stronger team.

Keeping your team balanced and focused on the critical issues while avoiding distractions can be important to effective execution. Our beloved dog Casey was a Jack Russell terrier. If you know the breed, you know them to be independent and strong-willed. She was totally obsessed with playing with a tennis ball and would run to fetch a tennis ball until she dropped from exhaustion if we let her. If offered two tennis balls at once, she would try to pick up both, but of course her mouth was too small to allow that. She struggled until she finally dropped one ball and then picked up the other. But she never realized that she was not capable of carrying two tennis balls at once, so she kept trying. It was fun to watch. Know your capabilities and how many tennis balls you can carry. Trading one perfectly good tennis ball for another may not be a good investment of time and effort. Maybe it's better to be happy with the tennis ball you have and play with it as best you can!

An effective way to assess how well your team is executing is to look for the little failures. Big failures are usually rare, so searching for the big failures is often fruitless. Little failures happen every day and are easy to find and even to fix. It's like the saying, "Take care of the pennies, and the dollars take care of themselves." If your team is failing to execute the little things well, there is a good chance they are also failing at the big things, but you don't know it. The other issue is that those little failures, under adverse conditions, can become big failures. We never know which one of these pesky little failures will become the big failure that we dread, but eventually one of them will.

> Do or do not … there is no try.
> —Master Yoda

Being a Great Leader

Do you want to be a great leader? Here are a few pointers.

- Create a *vision* and communicate it in all you say and especially in all you do.
- Be *passionate* about your work. Take *ownership* of the results, not just the activities.
- *Care* about and support your people. Help them be successful. Do not permit failure.
- Maintain consistent high *integrity* in all your activities. Be authentic, not perfect.
- *Challenge* yourself and others to learn from the work every day.
- *Execute*—recognize the good work and ask for improvement when needed.
- Have *fun* and make work fun for others.

Summary of Balance in Leadership

We introduced the concept of the decision point—the optimal balance point between conflicting elements with associated costs and benefits. The balance point is a dynamic point, constantly changing as conditions around us change. The challenge for the leader is to search constantly for the optimal balance in their behavior and then to adjust to it as best they can, recognizing that perfection is neither possible nor affordable. Ride the multidimensional bicycle and don't allow failure.

No two leaders will choose the same decision point, even under similar circumstances. Authentic leaders choose decision points that are consistent and authentic with who they are. To do otherwise would be unauthentic and inconsistent. I am trained as a chemist, and one of the foundational concepts of chemistry is that atoms and molecules are in a constant state of dynamic equilibrium—always changing even when the appearance is static. The only true stasis is when there is an equal number of molecules moving up as there are moving down. This appears to be an unchanging situation at the macro level, but at the molecular level, there is a tremendous amount of activity going on all the time. The same is true in leadership. People are always changing, the economy is always changing, markets are always changing, consumers are always changing, our competitors are always changing, and so on. To expect stasis is foolish. Therefore, as leaders, we must be attuned to the changes around us that will impact the decision points we choose and use this to dynamically adjust our actions and behavior as appropriate. We are going to be busy!

Chapter 2

Balance in Leading Yourself

Leading yourself is about you. Your attitude, your behavior, your demeanor, how you take care of yourself, and even how you dress impact your performance as a leader. In this chapter, we will consider some of the elements that are important in successfully leading yourself. This doesn't mean that there is a right or a wrong way, only that there are elements you will need to balance. If you are unable to lead yourself, you will have a difficult time leading others. If your behavior is inconsistent with what you say, you will confuse people. You need to be in balance too.

Your Mission, Vision, and Values

The first step in leading yourself is to understand your personal mission, vision, and values. If you were a building, your mission, vision, and values would be the foundation. The foundation needs to be a solid and cohesive whole that can support the rest of the structure, including how we relate to and lead the groups of which we are a part. We start here because everything else that follows is based on this. We cannot establish balance without a solid footing, or we will be constantly searching for direction.

Your mission is what you do—why you get out of bed in the morning. Your vision is what you want to achieve at some future date. Your values are the ideals that you strive for now and into the future. You will not compromise your values to achieve your mission or vision. Your mission and vision will change with time. Your values, by contrast, will not change substantially over your entire career or even life.

It is important for us to be aware of and live by our values. You make decisions based on your mission and vision, while your behavior is based on your values. People who do not know or do not honor their values behave inconsistently. People know you by your values. We talked about the importance of authenticity in a leader. Authenticity requires being true to your values. Our values keep us grounded on the ideals that are important to us, so we don't drift during difficult times. We do not want to balance or compromise our values. Of course, people evolve over long periods of time, so our ideals can change, but in the short term, barring a life-changing event, values are usually stable. Our values are the foundation on which we build our careers and our lives.

My personal values include being dependable, constantly learning, constantly challenging the status quo, constantly improving, making progress, teaching others, having fun, and never having to regret what I have done. These are the ideals that drive me to behave the way I do every minute of every day. If you work with me, you may wonder, *Why does Len always ask tough questions at meetings?* If you know my values, then you wouldn't be surprised because you know that it would kill me to sit quietly when I have a challenging question to ask, especially when I think it could help us improve our performance. This situation involves two of my personal values—challenging the status quo and constantly improving. And while asking that tough question, I'd probably involve another of my personal values by asking the question in a joking manner—in order to have some fun while doing it!

An important value for a leader to have is integrity, and it would seem as if there was no place for balance in choosing how much integrity to have. Your integrity is your word and bond and is not to be compromised. You build trust in relationships based on others' perception of your integrity. It takes many positive encounters to build trust and one negative encounter to destroy it. Maintaining your integrity can be costly. Others may appreciate your consistent integrity and dependability, but some are bound to think you are inflexible or unchanging. For example, being honest does not mean saying everything that is on your mind or, worse, on the tip of your tongue. Discretion is not the opposite of integrity but rather allows us to maintain integrity while not offending others around us. We are entitled to our opinions and often must keep them to ourselves. It may come as a surprise to us that others do not see the world as we do. We each have a unique perspective, and imposing or insisting on our view of the world is not integrity; it is coercion.

The company we work for will have a set of values that are likely different from, but hopefully not inconsistent with, our personal values. If you are unable to align with the company values, you will need to compromise your personal values, and you will be unhappy. Typical business values might include being involved in the community, environmental stewardship, fairness in dealing with vendors, providing value to our customers, competing fairly in the marketplace, complying with all regulations, meeting or exceeding the expectations of our customers, and delivering a profit to our shareholders. A good practice is to write our values out and post them in a conspicuous spot to remind us of them often.

When we are having a tough day or making a difficult decision, it helps to remind ourselves of our values and the company values. Missions and visions, on the other hand, are rather changeable. Not that we want to change these often, but they can and should change in the light of new opportunity. I have always wanted to be an inventor, and maybe someday I will be, but when the opportunity came to work as a product developer in a bakery, I took it and made a career of it. Getting used to eating and having a roof over your head and clothes on your back has a way of convincing you to change your mission and vision. Missions and visions have to pass a practicality test. They need to be achievable and meaningful.

I used to ask people at job interviews and training classes what they wanted to be doing in five years. I was hoping they would tell me, "I want to be a plant manager" or "I want to be working in research," or any other definitive career option. Rarely did I get a clear or definitive response. At first, I thought it was because the candidates were listless or did not have a mission or vision. They couldn't tell me what job they wanted to be doing in five years, and as I learned from this experience, it was an unfair expectation. The fact of the matter is that most of us get a job, learn about the work that is available, and then take opportunities as they come to us. We tend to bounce around the organization awhile as long as we are reasonably challenged, learning, advancing, getting paid, and having some fun. When any of these falter or we start to stagnate, we either find another job to get back on track or we settle in for the long haul and coast the rest of our careers. It is such a waste for us to sit back and coast at any time in our careers. However, it is easy for us and the organization we are working for to do so. We know the job and can do it with our eyes closed. The organization is happy that we are doing the job well, and no one has to worry about us; they can close their eyes too. That is the time to reassess your mission and vision and set new ones that are challenging and appropriate to your current situation. Leaders need a vision of where they want to take people. Dreaming about what could be is a good way to discover this place. Dreams can be motivational, giving a long-term or bigger purpose and meaning to our work and our lives, helping us get through tough times. Dreaming is not usually considered a good thing to do at work, but of course I don't mean the kind of dreaming that we do when we're sleeping. I'm talking about the kind of dreaming we do when we envision or imagine what success would look like. I like the word *dreaming* better than *imagining,* as I think dreaming is more unfettered. When I imagine a better world, I put my ideas into the context of my current reality with a little liberty to go beyond reality, but when I dream, I don't allow reality to constrain my thinking. I am free to create a new reality that is not constrained by my current reality. And that is what I want to do—dream of a situation that is successful beyond my wildest imagination. In this context, dreaming can be a powerful way to jump from a problem to a potential long-term solution. Reality has a way of blocking our view of what can be, constraining our efforts by forcing us to be too shortsighted or too focused on the here and now. Some people call this "the box" and suggest that we need to think outside the box, whereas Jeff Bezos says, "Why think outside the box. What box?"

Sometimes we need to step back from the situation to get enough perspective to see the mountains beyond the hills that we are working on. The real gold is in those mountains. Stop, step away from the problem, and envision what success would look and feel like. Some questions that can help include the following:

- What is there that I cannot currently do, but if I could, it would change everything? (That is one powerful question!)
- If the problem was solved, what would be happening?
- How would the world be different?
- Identify concrete differences—not just "people would care." What does it mean that people would care?
- Why would they care?
- How would their behavior be different?
- Why would they behave differently?
- What does success look like?

Those who dream with their eyes open are dangerous people as they work in the daylight to make their dreams come true.
—Alexander Pope

I'm pretty sure that birds don't dream about their future. When our kids were young, we took a vacation in Las Vegas, and one day, we drove into Death Valley. It is a surreal and beautiful place. It was also 135 degrees Fahrenheit and windy. It was like being inside a convection oven. We stopped at a small store to buy some drinks. Outside was a small, lone palm tree. Standing in the tiny spot of shade under this straggly palm tree were two bedraggled crows, with their beaks open, panting to cool off. We felt sorry for them, so I told them to fly over the mountains into Las Vegas where there was water and beautiful gardens. Of course, they didn't move, as they didn't understand me, nor could they even dream that only a short flight away was such a beautiful place as Vegas. They stayed where they were and suffered in the heat and dust. Like these poor crows, we can fall victim to a suboptimal present if we fail to dream about a better future that could be lurking just over those hills that surround us and make us believe that this is all there is for us in life.

As a leader, you need to sell your vision to your team. "I'm the boss, so I don't have to sell my ideas to people; I pay them to do what I expect them to do." True but wrong! You don't need to act like a salesman, but you need to sell. You need to sell the message, and they must buy it in order for the team to be successful. Communicate the vision in all you say and do, every day. Be aware of the balance you are striking. Be authentic and reasonable. Be consistent but flexible. Be passionate and sincere. Challenge and support your people to success. Have fun and make it fun. That is how you sell the vision and get your team to buy into it and make it their vision. Sell it!

How do we create a new mission or vision for ourselves, our teams, or our company? Consider your values and the options available. Maybe you can find a way to make your current job more exciting by setting a new and challenging vision for yourself. One of my favorite questions is "What needs to be done?" Notice how different this is from "What do I want to do?" The first is a more important and motivating question—and actually much easier to find an answer to.

- Are you creating and taking opportunities to improve every day by asking, "What needs to be done?"
- Are you learning something new every day?
- Can you find a way to do your job better today than yesterday?
- Are you growing as a person?
- Are you stagnating in your job, or are you changing and growing your job?

Setting and going after a specific and challenging vision can be significant in driving our performance and our lives. Balance the risk of failing versus the risk of missing an opportunity.

The greater danger for most of us
is not that we aim too high and miss it
but that we aim too low and reach it.
—Michelangelo

Emotional Intelligence

Emotional intelligence is about being aware of our emotions and effectively managing our behaviors, sometimes in spite of our emotions. Emotions and feelings are unavoidable, even negative ones. However, the behaviors we choose based on these emotions and feelings are not unavoidable. We can choose good or bad behaviors. The balance we strike in this choice will be important.

One way to look at emotional intelligence is that it is about accepting responsibility for our behaviors. Or as my dear mentor Dr. Charles Stewart called it, "respons-ability," emphasizing that we are able to respond appropriately and are responsible for doing so. We cannot just say, "You made me mad." No one can "make" you mad. You actually decide to become mad in response to a situation that you don't like. Too bad! You may not be able to control the situation, and you may not be able to control your feelings, but you can manage your reaction. Blaming someone else for how we behave is an abdication of responsibility for our own selves. I love when Tony Soprano screams at the dead body he is standing over, "Look what you made me do!" He obviously hadn't heard about emotional intelligence.

We are wired for emotions and cannot help but feel emotions in response to life's events, both positive and negative. We do not, however, need to be subject to our emotions, especially the negative ones like anger or fear, without any ability to manage our responses. My friend Dr. Ross Ellis and his compatriots Dr. Darwin Nelson and Dr. Gary Low teach that the first step is to be aware of your emotions and then to consider how you want to behave. It all happens so fast, almost automatically, that we may think that we cannot control our reaction, but this is where the intelligence part comes in. We want to develop an awareness of how we react to our emotions and have the ability to consider our response with our cognitive mind to make sure that the response is appropriate. We will not stop or change the emotion we feel; that is wired into our brains and based on past experiences we probably don't even remember anymore. The idea is not to control our emotions but rather to manage our actions. Dr. Ellis tells us first to be aware of the emotion we are feeling, then wait about six seconds while we feel the emotion and consider how to react in a positive manner. The balance comes in being able to act intelligently and not emotionally. Balancing our desire to react with our desire to react appropriately is a simple concept and an important one in our personal development journey. The emotion is still there; we just choose how to act positively as opposed to reacting negatively. This is not as easy as it sounds and takes some conscious effort, practice, and time.

A special skill in emotional intelligence is the ability to keep calm and effectively manage our emotions in the midst of a conflict. When others are losing their tempers and exhibiting a lack of self-management, it is to our benefit to maintain our balance and demonstrate effective self-management. We are better able to assess the situation from a position of calm neutrality and may be able to avoid getting caught up in the emotion of the moment. A good example is when someone is attacking us verbally. Maintaining our composure can be an effective way to handle the attacker. Empathize with them by saying, "I understand" or "I hear what you're saying." You do not need to agree with them unless you actually do. If you can ask a question, do so. People cannot avoid answering a question in their head, and it will usually cause them to think for a second and may help break the irrational outburst. This is a good opportunity for you to observe them and see how committed they are to the issue. If they have lost their composure and we have not, they will be confused or embarrassed, and they may stop the verbal attack when they realize that they are the ones making all the noise. They will eventually calm down and match our demeanor if they are reasonable people who want to get along. If they are unreasonable, they may escalate the pitch and go for double or nothing. They may realize that they are losing and will work twice as hard to get us to lose our temper and join them. Don't do it. Stay calm and observe them closely to see which way they go. Do not walk away, as this will infuriate them even more and make it look like you are running away. You want to deal with the situation now if possible, as they have a lot invested in this exchange and will want to have something to show for it, so you are actually in a good bargaining position—if they are reasonable. If they are truly unreasonable, then leaving may be the best option.

High emotion and tense feelings may result in us saying something that we will later regret. Once the words escape our lips, they are gone and cannot be retracted. The hurt or insult they cause will have a consequence for us at some point. Those words are not free. There is a price to be paid. Does this mean that we need to act like robots and always be cheerful in our responses? No, we don't want to be robots or cheerful idiots. If someone wrongs us, we want to be able to advise them of that fact and get them to at least understand that we are not happy with their behavior. Sometimes it's even okay to express anger. Anger expressed in a positive, managed fashion can be a powerful communicator. We don't want to overdo it or overuse anger, as we will get a bad reputation, and people will tune us out. But once in a while, it may be an effective response to let someone know we care and are upset with their behavior.

> Anyone can become angry—that is easy, but to be angry with the right person at the right time, and for the right purpose and in the right way—that is not within everyone's power and that is not easy.
>
> —Aristotle

It may seem like the purpose of emotional intelligence is to change us, rather than just change our behavior. But can we change—*really* change—who we are? To what extent is my behavior dependent or determined based on who I am? In other words, do I always have to act like me? My mentor Dr. Charlie Stewart teaches that we cannot change who we are, but we can augment our behaviors by consciously choosing new and more effective behaviors. If I am a builder, and the only tools I have in my toolbox are a hammer and a saw, then those are the tools I use in all situations, even when there are much better tools available. If I take the time to acquire and learn how to use a new tool, from that day forward, when a situation presents itself, I can choose to use the new and better tool in order to solve the issue more effectively. Learning a new behavior can do the same, by giving us a new tool for our toolbox that will be more effective than our old behavior. But be aware that there is always a risk; when the situation is tense or I am under stress, I may revert to using my old, familiar, less effective behavior. Deep down, it is still my default behavior, and by learning a new behavior, I do not unlearn the old behavior. It's still in my toolbox, waiting to be selected. Learning to use the new behavior hasn't changed me; it has just given me a new tool to use—if I choose to use it.

An example of the benefit of being emotionally intelligent is when we are set up by a boss or a peer. Eventually, you will encounter struggles over power or turf and will be the target of a setup. It will be a particularly difficult time for you to maintain your balance in order to react in an emotionally intelligent manner—and critically important that you do so. Surviving a setup will gain you respect or a new job! Perhaps your boss doesn't particularly like you or your style. Maybe you have been critical of them in the past and they have a score to settle, or they just want to get rid of you so they can replace you with someone more amenable to them. It is a common situation, and eventually in your career, you will have to deal with it. Sometimes these situations are not possible to win, and the best outcome may be to get a draw so that you can live to fight another day.

Here is an example of a setup and how the game is played— and it helps to keep in mind that it is a game. Your boss creates an inner circle of close confidants, and you are not one of them. Plans are made to do something, and at the last minute, they invite you to attend. You might already have other plans, but they expect you to change your plans to attend. You reluctantly decide to comply and prepare a presentation for the meeting as requested. At the meeting, of course, time is short, so they beg your forgiveness that there is unfortunately no time for you to present, or you have to severely cut short your presentation. This pattern goes on for a few weeks or months. You get annoyed and maybe say something about it, or you decide the next time it happens, you are not going to change your plans.

Next, they come to you and tell you that you are not being a team player and if you do not change your ways, there will be consequences. This is the "team player" setup. It is an easy setup to create and a very difficult one to defend. In fact, defending yourself will give them more ammunition to prove that you are not a team player and potentially make the situation worse. Your feelings are hurt; you are convinced that you are the victim and they are the aggressor. You defend or take the offensive, and you end up getting fired. They win; you lose. You have lost your balance.

How else can you play this game? Other options include saying nothing in response to their accusations—the Jesus approach. It didn't work too well for him, and it won't work too well for you either. The best and really only constructive approach is to empathize with them—not agree but acknowledge their contention that you have not been a team player. You don't need to agree, just acknowledge. This may throw them off balance a bit, and it will buy you some time. You say things like "I can see why you might think that" or "I understand what you are saying." Be patient and give them time to speak and say everything they want to say. You need to hear all the gory details of their accusation and listen for clues as to the source of their complaints against you. These could be useful pieces of information to help you plan your next constructive move. Listen carefully and do not interrupt them to defend yourself in any way. Keep empathizing and listening. Let them talk until they have nothing else to say. Then, after they sit in front of you silent for a full minute and have nothing else to say, say something like "I acknowledge what you are saying, and I will work on improving." Then shut up. This will take a lot of self-control on your part not to defend yourself or, worse, to attack them for the injustice they are foisting on you. Keep your cool and your balance and then take deliberate, measured steps to be a good team player. You will have a difficult time meeting their full demands, as they will make it difficult for you to do that, but you may be able to do enough to defuse and survive the attack. That is your goal—survival. Not winning— only survival. If you survive, you get to wait out the situation and buy enough time to make a decision that is constructive and good for you, as opposed to being reactive and bad for you. It may be time to change jobs or at least bosses. It may be a great time to ask for a transfer to a different department or location in the company for developmental purposes. This way, you retain your seniority, income, and benefits while escaping a bad situation and convert it into a good situation. Don't defend. Instead, maintain your cool, keep your balance, and act constructively and deliberately. That is only way I have learned to survive and even succeed in a setup.

Being emotionally intelligent can involve the effective use of our feelings as well. After all, our feelings are authentic and real. I once told a VP that his behavior "really pissed me off." It stopped him dead in his tracks, and he wanted to know what he had done. He listened to my explanation and changed his behavior. The best part is that we became friends with a greater level of respect for each other that impacted our relationship going forward in a positive manner. The reason this communication worked so well is that it was a sincere, deeply felt expression of my real feelings. It was directed at the other person's behavior and did not attack them as a person. It's very difficult for someone to deny your expression of how you are feeling. If you tell me you are feeling confused, empowered, abandoned, welcome, or anything else, who am I to doubt or deny your feeling? A sincere expression of what you are feeling in a situation is a powerful communication. The feeling you describe must be in response to the other person's behavior or the situation they have created—not about them as a person. This keeps the communication from becoming a personal attack. The purpose is to make them aware of how I feel when they behave in a certain way. The balance to be struck in communicating feelings is toward the "once in a blue moon" end of the scale. It is powerful but if overused will lose its effectiveness and gain you a reputation of being a whiner. Communicate your feelings only when there is no other way to make your point. It can be a great way to deal with someone who is much stronger than you are. Use it carefully!

Smart and Wise

Do you know the difference between being smart and wise? They are not the same. It's difficult to be both smart and wise at the same time. The individuals who can strike a balance between these are indeed rare and interesting people. They are our most charismatic and powerful leaders.

Smart is knowing the facts and being sharp, mentally alert, mentally quick, resourceful, and so on. There are people who are walking encyclopedias. Ask them the temperature of the sun or the migration pattern of the monarch butterfly, and they are sure to know the answer—definitively. And they are probably right. These people take pride in knowing the answer to everything. It is their job to search for fun facts everywhere and all the time. There is nothing wrong with this; it is actually a great way to keep a superior intellect busy and sharp. And that is what these people are—bright, energetic, and inquisitive with great memories and a strong need to impress themselves and others with how brilliant they are. Sorry—did that sound negative? Well, these people can be a bore to the rest of us mortals who don't care how many bosons are in a gluon (that is totally wrong, and I don't care!).

How do you know if you are one of these people? When someone asks a question on any subject, do you find yourself rushing to be the first in the room to express the answer? When you're in a room, do you always feel like you are the smartest person in the room—in your unbiased opinion of course? Being smart is important in today's world. Knowing facts can make you an expert or a go-to person on the staff. Being smart and knowledgeable is good. Just be careful not to be obsessed with being the smartest person around all the time. You may not know it, but if that is how you feel, it will be obvious in your behavior to everyone else in the room. And some of them may not agree with your assessment! Acting too smart can alienate you from other people, so be smart, in balance!

Working for a boss who thinks they are the smartest or wisest person around can be an interesting challenge. They will not appreciate your attempts to show how smart or wise you are, because it may show them up. Their need to be the smartest or wisest is probably based on a deep-seated neurosis, so their actions may appear illogical or inconsistent with what they say. These people can be great bosses to work for, but every now and then, they will not be able to control their need to be the smartest or the wisest, and you will get squashed. It doesn't mean they hate you or feel any differently about your contribution to the organization. It just means they had to feed their ego this time. Get over it and chalk it up to experience. The other issue with a boss who thinks they know it all is that when you are talking to them about your brilliant idea, they may say, "Wow. This is great. Tell me more." They give the impression of being open to you, when they are actually gathering more facts about your idea, which they will use to squash it when the time comes. You will feel betrayed by the event and sulk back to your cubical, but remember their need. Depending on how often they feed their need, you can decide if it is worth the trouble.

As a leader, you need smart people to help you get the job done. Are you willing and able to hire people who are smarter than you? Is that even possible? If you always think you are the smartest person around, then by definition you will not find someone who is smarter than you are. Of course, there are lots of people out there who are smarter than we are in one aspect or another. I don't want to conduct a psychological study here, but it helps to understand what motivates us. Most extreme behaviors like the need to be the smartest, biggest, baddest, and so on are motivated by a neurosis. Somewhere back in our childhood, we were hurt by a parent, a peer, a sibling, a teacher, or some authority figure, and we found a way to survive and get the at-a-boy we wanted so badly. We found that by being smart and knowing the facts, we got rewards. The behavior was reinforced and strengthened by rewards. Today, that same tape is playing in our heads: if you want rewards, then be smart. It worked back when we were kids, and our brain still thinks it will work today even though we are no longer kids. And sometimes it does work, and the reinforcement continues, mostly. The risk is that we don't see the damage that is caused by being driven to be the smartest all the time. If I have a need to be the smartest person around, I probably will not hire someone who I fear is smarter than me because it could threaten my position as the smartest person. Or worse, if I do hire a smarter person, I may spend all my efforts to prove that I am smarter in the end. Destructive behaviors all—we need some wisdom to balance our smarts!

Wisdom is different from being smart. Wisdom is the ability to assess a situation, see the pros and cons of potential actions, and make a good decision based on incomplete or even contradictory information. I said "good" and not "right" for a reason. A good decision is the best decision I can make with the facts and the situation as it stands. It may not be the right decision as more facts become available or the situation changes. How is it possible to make a good decision when the facts at hand are incomplete or even wrong? That is the key question. If you are smart and use all the incomplete and wrong facts at hand and good logical processes, you will either burn yourself out, because you cannot come to a decision, or you will make a bad decision based on the bad facts. A smart person must know the facts, and to them, the facts are immutable, and logic dictates how to make a decision based on the facts. You can see where this is going. Watch how "smart" people chase their tails or never seem to be able to make a decision. Their statements are full of facts and reasoning, but they don't get anywhere. A decision based only on facts can change radically if one of the "facts" changes. These people can be seen as flip-floppers because it looks like they are always changing their minds. A fact may have changed, causing them to rerun their decision analysis, and this time the logic dictates a different decision. Since they are totally committed to the process rather than the result, their values force them to change their decision. Process is important and useful, but a decision should never be dictated by the process alone. If you like processes and facts, be prepared to flip-flop as facts evolve.

A wise person, on the other hand, sizes up a situation by considering the facts on hand, but in addition, they consider their values and goals. They discount facts that appear inconsistent, incomplete, or wrong, and then they make a decision. They express their decision in the context of their values and goals. They won't always get the decision part perfectly right, as the facts may be incomplete or wrong, but the values and goals are solid. Changing facts will have no impact on their values or goals, so they usually don't have to change their decisions when facts evolve. These people can be perceived as stubborn or inflexible by people who observe that the facts have changed, but there is no consequent change in the decision. This makes no sense to them. They do not see that the underlying foundation of values and goals is the real basis for the decision. The changing facts are mosquitoes that hover and annoy but are not consequential to the decision.

> To attain knowledge, add things every day.
> To attain wisdom, remove things every day.
> —Tao Te Ching

One way to be smart and not act like a know-it-all is to ask questions. When the group is going in the wrong direction or missing an important angle on a situation, ask them an open question about it. "Have we considered the opportunity cost of the Smith project? We'll have 30 percent of our resources tied up for two years and may have to turn away other higher potential projects that come along." This can get the group thinking. It's better than saying, "The Smith project will tie up 30 percent of our resources for two years, resources that we could apply to more profitable projects." Watch other people's faces when you ask them a question. They cannot help but think about it to look for an answer. Watch when you tell them an unpleasant statement they don't want to hear; they tune it out. It's very difficult to tune out a question. They may ignore you, but at least you made them think.

What the wise do in the beginning, fools do in the end.
—Warren Buffett

Where does wisdom come from? This is a question that many have struggled with. It appears that as we age and gather experience, we can become wiser. Yet there are some very young people who are naturally wise, and we probably know some people who have been around awhile but still are not wise. Age and experience are factors but not necessarily causal to wisdom. A challenging life with varied experiences can build wisdom if it doesn't cause us to become bitter or cynical. Experience certainly builds a broader perspective from which to judge situations. The way we use facts when making a decision seems to be the real differentiator between being smart and being wise. Be careful to put facts into context and discard unreliable or inconsistent facts. Consider your mission, vision, and values at all times and make your decisions consistent with those, even if the facts dictate otherwise. That is true wisdom.

Risking Your Job to Save It

Laurie Beth Jones wrote a great little book called *Jesus, CEO*,[4] and in it she applies the teachings of Jesus to the context of a modern work environment. It is well written and certainly a different and interesting approach to the subject. There is one of Jesus's teachings that she does not discuss in her book, but I wish that she had, so please permit me to add it. Jesus said, "To save your life, you must lose it." In other words, we must be willing to risk our lives to help others, or we will become selfish and closed to the needs of those around us, and we will not gain salvation. I paraphrase this, as she might have done, for leadership as "To save your job, you must risk it."

To me, this means that we cannot always take the safe way out. We must unavoidably balance the risks in the decisions we make with the potential benefits to the actions we take. We do not want to be foolish and take meaningless risks, but some risks are worth it. Is it risky to point out to your boss that they may be on the wrong path? You bet it can be risky. Do you think it's risky to project next year's performance at 7 percent better than this year? Is it risky to invest in new equipment or hire new people? There is risk in everything we do and do not do. The difference between a successful and an unsuccessful person is often in the size of the risks they take and their execution of those decisions. Committing to and delivering a 4 percent sales increase next year is safer than stretching for 7 percent, but the difference over several years is the difference between a good performance and a great performance. The balance that we strike between safety and risk is potentially a consequential one.

As a leader, you need to be willing and capable of displaying some balls, guts, intestinal fortitude, courage, or whatever we want to call it. This can be risky, but it can also give people reason to have confidence in you as a leader. People will not follow a person who has no spine. At times, you will need to appropriately display persistence, commitment, ownership, caring, risk taking, saying what you think is right, strength, self-confidence, fearlessness, integrity, and so on, in spite of the risks that accompany these behaviors.

Most of the promotions I got in my career I got because I stood up and told my boss what I thought was right, even when it wasn't popular at the time. My rule is simple: if I don't know what I'm talking about, I won't say a word, but if I'm sure I am right, I will find a way to express my opinion. As the team discusses a situation and works toward making a decision, I have a choice—do I speak up or keep silent? I always let other people speak first and allow them to get their ideas out. I avoid dominating the discussion. If I am sure about my perspective on the situation, when my turn comes, I will speak up and persist in doing so. Not in a domineering manner but persistently. On the other hand, I suggest that if you are not sure of the facts or what to do, keep quiet. I like the old saying, "If you don't know, it's better to keep quiet and not let anyone know you are ignorant than to open your mouth and prove it."

Speaking your mind when you are certain of your facts and ideas can be a career-changing moment—good or bad. Remember that our bosses need smart people who are willing and able to make decisions and lead the organization. Sometimes the fact that you stepped up to the plate on an issue will get you some good attention from the boss. You are demonstrating one of the signs of a leader; you have considered the situation and are not afraid to get out in front of the team to express your thoughts. Bosses are not omniscient, and often they are open to different ideas. On the other hand, no boss likes to hear an opinion that is contrary to their own. That is simply human nature. There will be a consequence and a price to pay for your persistence, and sometimes it is worth the price. Good bosses will at least listen to a contrary opinion, and if they are an enlightened leader, they may even adopt it. Don't expect your boss to always be enlightened. And keep in mind that the boss may have information about the situation that has not been shared with you. Therefore, when they reject your brilliant advice, maybe, just maybe, they know something you don't know, and they might be right. Speak your piece and then shut up! Don't make a fool of yourself, going down in flames in order to defend your suggestion to the end.

Consider how comfortable you are in a situation to determine if you have chosen the right balance between risk and safety. Chances are if you feel safe and comfortable, then you are not taking enough risks! Perhaps you are probably not pushing yourself or your team to improve. "If you want to change something, you have to change something," Yogi Berra says. Another quote I like is "Different is not always better, but better is always different." This comes from Dale Dauten, a noted author on creativity. He is absolutely right. If you are feeling comfortable in your current position, you are likely not changing. And if you are not changing, you are not getting better. And if you are not getting better, you are going to be uncomfortable in the long run!

Bosses and organizations need good people who are willing to stand up and fight for what is right. If you are working for a boss who doesn't appreciate your input, even when you are right, chances are you're working for the wrong person. You need to leave for your own sanity and advancement. If you are working in an organization where they appreciate diverse opinions and people who stand up for what is right, then do so carefully and judiciously. Pick your opportunities carefully and work within the organization to be heard and to get others to join you. Being a renegade is a foolish risk and not likely to succeed. Having a different opinion and convincing others by building a consensus around the different opinion will work and get you noticed by management as a true team player and an effective leader.

> If you are not prepared to resign or be fired for
> what you believe in, then you are not a worker,
> let alone a professional. You are a slave.
> —Howard Gardner

Adequacy and Inadequacy

Do you sometimes feel as though you are inadequate for the task or job you are given? Are you sometimes not sure if your work is good enough? Maybe you're not getting enough positive feedback to confirm that your work is meeting the requirements. How do you deal with these feelings?

I'll let you in on a secret. We all have feelings of inadequacy occasionally. Even top managers have these feelings. In fact, top management may be more prone to these feelings, as they often are isolated and get little or no feedback from their boss and certainly none of a critical or constructive nature from their subordinates. How do we maintain our balance when we feel inadequate or unsure of our performance? Looking for evidence and asking a trusted peer are options. Mostly, we need to get past our negative feelings and keep working. Do your best at all times. If your best is not good enough, then you have to find a way to improve beyond your best performance. You should not ignore your feelings, as feelings are a good source of information; that is probably why we have them. If your performance is truly inadequate in the eyes of others or your boss, you want to know this and deal with it in a constructive manner. However, you do not want your feelings to derail your performance. Being aware of your feelings and dealing with them in a thoughtful and constructive manner is important to your well-being and your performance.

On the other side of that coin, it is wise not to get too comfortable. It is good to be watchful and aware of negative reactions and words from others. People will sometimes drop a hint of negative feedback. Remember that they are likely reluctant to tell you the whole story. In a situation where they don't like something you did, they won't say what they really think, but they may not be able to allow the opportunity to go by without saying something, so they drop a hint or a look. Sometimes your perceptions are good indicators that something is wrong and you need to reassess the situation. Here are the three worst, and usually wrong, perceptions to watch out for:

- I'm no good. (You're probably much better than you give yourself credit for.)
- I feel sorry for myself. (Self-pity is not pretty and is self-destructive.)
- No one else knows anything. I'm the only smart person here. (Not likely.)

These are red flags that your thinking is out of touch with reality. You need to ground yourself in some real data. Do you have a friend or peer you can talk to and trust? Another great option is to find someone who has experience in your area and ask them to be your mentor. Ask them to give you some feedback. We all can benefit from having a mentor we trust and can talk to about almost anything.

Andy Grove, the former CEO of Intel, wrote a book titled *Only the Paranoid Survive.*[5] It is a great book. I gave a copy to one of my direct reports who had a can-do attitude but often underestimated potential issues, resulting in failed or late projects. I advised him to read this book but then revised my advice to suggest that he just read the table of contents. And then I realized that he could get the point of the book just by reading the title! We want to achieve a reasonable assessment of the risks and benefits, on balance, avoiding over- and underestimation. Overestimating the issues and difficulty of a project can cause project paralysis, with nothing getting done because we never get all the stars aligned to our satisfaction. Underestimating the issues and difficulty of a project might make us look good until the stuff hits the fan and we have no good plan B to bail ourselves out. A proper dose of paranoia can be healthy, in balance, to alert us to potential risks, so that we can take constructive steps to avoid failure while at the same time putting together a good contingency plan, in case failure occurs. Too much paranoia, however, can result in paralysis. We can get so tied up considering all the possible bad consequences that we fail to take any action at all. In balance, a little healthy paranoia can be good, while none or a lot are likely bad.

Above all, don't fester in these negative and destructive feelings. You will become known as a bitter and negative person, and other people will avoid you. Find a way to refute those negative feelings, turn them into positive thinking, and get on with your life. Read a book on positive thinking, like those written by Tony Robbins or Napoleon Hill—both great writers on the subject. Pay attention to your feelings and assess the possibility that there is a problem, and then move on, adjusting your plan if needed. This, of course, is much easier to say than do. You must be your own best cheerleader and supporter—just in case no one else is!

Asking Questions

A powerful way to keep in balance as a person and as a leader is to ask lots of questions. Ask yourself questions to keep yourself in balance and to make sure your goals are high enough. Ask your team members questions to get the feedback you need and to make sure you are in touch with their issues, needs, feelings, and challenges. Don't ask your boss too many questions, unless you already know the answer! Your boss expects you to bring them answers, not questions.

Here are some questions that I like to ask myself every morning as I plan my day:

- What is the most important thing I can work on today?
- What do I want to accomplish today? Make a reasonable list and commit to getting it done.
- Am I leading in balance? Where am I out of balance?
- Am I getting the results that I want?
- Am I taking care of myself and my team?
- Am I developing my skills and the skills of my team members?
- Am I challenging myself and my team appropriately?
- Am I giving my team members enough positive feedback and recognition?
- What are the potential trade-offs and consequences of my actions or inaction today?

Ask yourself and your team lots of questions. Questions make you and your team members think. Thinking is good. We spend too little time thinking. Are you asking the right questions? Are you satisfied with the answers? What is the reason for asking the question in the first place? Is it to get information? How about to challenge people to do better or consider other options? The best way to do this is to ask questions in a way that avoids putting them on the defensive. Asking a question is a great way to challenge people and get them to think about the options.

Dr. Phil asks one great question, "How is that working for you?" This question stops a complaining, ranting tirade in its tracks, as the person stops to consider how to respond. It also forces them to realize the truth—their behavior is not working out so well. Why then am I so committed to it? Why have I invested so much energy in it? Why do I continue to invest more energy in it if it's not giving me the result that I want? It's a great nonoffensive, thought-provoking question. How is that working for you?

Asking questions is an art form. Questions can be constructive and inquisitive or judgmental and hurtful. Avoid the use of negative words in the questions you ask—*why, should, you need, you, my,* and so on. Note that "I need" or "we need" are okay; only "you need" is to be avoided. Instead of asking, "Why are sales in your region down 5 percent?" consider "What are the reasons for the recent 5 percent sales decline that we are seeing?" Instead of "Why do you need to spend three days on the Smith project?" consider "How was it determined to spend three days on the Smith project?" Saying "we" instead of "I" or "you" reduces the tension in the question.

Learning

Learning is an important and underappreciated skill. The ability to change and improve depends on learning. Learning is not just about learning new things but also unlearning old ideas that are no longer viable. The world is changing at a faster pace every year, making it more critical to unlearn and relearn more quickly as well. Maintaining your balance as a leader depends on your ability to adjust and change as the situation changes. This requires learning.

> Consistency requires you to be as ignorant
> today as you were a year ago.
> —Bernard Berenson

Learning, like most developmental activities, follows an S curve. At the start of a new project or job, the learning curve is steep as we are exposed to many new ideas and facts. Over time, the learning curve levels off and even plateaus to stagnation. The astute learner knows this and finds a way to branch off on a new S curve. Consider where you are on the learning S curve. Are you still actively learning in your job, or have you plateaued? Are you creating learning situations for yourself and your team as part of your everyday work? This means experimenting with different techniques to improve on past good results and of course improving on past not-so-good results. We seldom take time from our busy schedules to attend a training seminar or read a book, so our skills may stagnate.

- When did you last spend the time and effort to learn a new skill or technique?
- What if we incorporated learning opportunities in the work we do every day?
- What would happen if we leveraged our daily activities in order to learn and improve?
- How fast and how far could we improve if we made it a daily priority?
- How fast and far could our team improve if we made learning part of their daily goals?

The seemingly small, incremental, daily improvements compound like money in the bank and over time can result in a substantial change. The trick is to make learning part of your daily work. Next time you need to create an Excel spreadsheet, make a point of using a new command or technique. We can always manage to spend five or ten minutes a day learning, if we make it a point to do so. Learning how to learn is a critical skill to develop. Making learning part of the work we do every day can be a game changer for us.

> The illiterate of the future will not be the person who cannot read, it will be the person who does not know how to learn.
> —Alvin Toffler

My former boss Irwin Cooper used to ask, "How many years has Bob been with us?" If the answer was ten years, he would go further and ask, "Is that ten years or one year ten times?" What Irwin knew from experience was that for many people, the learning curve is steepest when they first take a new job, and then the curve flattens out, meaning after a few years, they are not learning or improving much—if at all. We don't want to allow ourselves or our people to stay on the flat part of the learning curve. We probably could not stand being on the steepest part every day either. The decision point will depend on the person, how ambitious we or they are, and what our goals are. When you reach a goal, set a new one and get going on a new learning curve.

> I know of no more encouraging fact than the unquestionable ability of man to elevate his life by conscious endeavor.
> —Henry David Thoreau

Great leaders find ways to grow as people and as leaders. Friends of Abraham Lincoln, on seeing him after a separation of several years, remarked on how he had grown as a person and as a leader. The difference was significant. He had not attended a seminar or read a self-help book. What he did was spend time every day building his skills and overcoming his weaknesses. Lincoln had very little formal education—intermittent perhaps to what we today would call sixth grade. He suffered from severe depression and great personal loss. He failed several times in business and in politics. In spite of these issues, he taught himself to be a lawyer, a politician, a great orator, and perhaps our greatest president, leading the country through its most difficult time. He did this through persistent hard work to learn and improve himself. He was a voracious reader. He communicated his vision (equality for all humanity) and trumped many more experienced politicians with his simple authenticity. Lincoln rose from a humble beginning to meet the challenges of his day by learning at an early age how to learn and develop his skills. Anticipate what skills you will need to be successful in the near future and then find ways to develop those skills in yourself and in your team.

Ignorance is a voluntary misfortune.
—Nicholas Ling

Do you view learning as an activity that you engage in actively or as something that happens to you, perhaps against your will? Do you want to learn, or are you forced to learn? Do you learn or expect to be trained? The model for education in the US is largely a push model, with students required to learn certain topics and skills. When we come to work, we apply the same learning model—that learning is a push (we call it training and development). We attend seminars when our boss sends us. At review time, we are told by our boss about our deficiencies, and they put together a plan for how we will improve, often without our involvement. Training is crammed down our throats whether we want it or not. This takes away self-initiative and ownership. Learning, like any other activity, is accomplished more effectively if led by a mission and vision, rather than pushed by someone else's agenda. A push model will not be very effective. Who forced Abe Lincoln to teach himself to be a lawyer? He set a mission and vision for himself and took the initiative and ownership to make it happen. We need to do the same for ourselves and for our direct reports. How about our children? Can we define a mission and vision for their learning that will allow them to take responsibility for their own education?

Learning happens best when we take personal responsibility for the process. We will not learn much if we take a passive role and wait for learning to happen to us. We need to take an active role and think. Consider the situation. What do you know, or think you know? What do you know that you don't know? What will you need to know? Ask questions. Observe the situation and ask more questions. Put what you know into a mental model. Use the mental model to identify what is missing from your expertise or knowledge. Then go find the answers and ask more questions. Keep doing this iteratively until your model is reasonably successful at describing reality.

Who trains a baby how to walk? No one. Babies learn how to walk. I'm certain that our doting helicopter parents of today would enroll their babies in special training sessions on how to walk if they existed. The fact is that it is neither possible nor necessary to train a baby to walk. They must learn on their own by falling and trying again and again repeatedly until they finally figure it out. Once they have learned how, it is impossible for them to unlearn it. They go in one step from staggering and being unbalanced to walking. My son seemed to go from holding onto the couch to running down the hall in one step. We don't think he ever walked! It is the same with learning any other skill.

Training can help only to the extent that it gives us the basics and can shorten the learning curve, but there is no way to replace the need for active learning. Instead of training, consider developing people by offering them opportunities to learn, such as an internship that would challenge their skills. We should create situations where our people can learn. These situations should be carefully designed to allow them to experiment and test their skills in an environment where failure is either possible, meaning not a serious event, or impossible, meaning that we provide a safety net to catch them and correct the situation before a serious failure occurs. In these ways, we can create an artificial environment where they feel safe to make mistakes and learn, just like a baby learning how to walk.

Russell Ackoff describes five levels of human mental processing that result in learning:

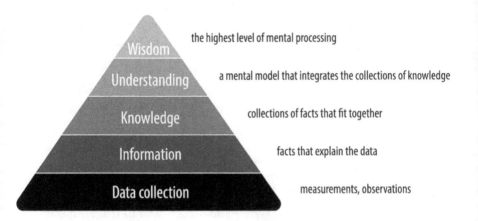

Dr. Ackoff's learning model[6] is rich and instructive for those of us who want to learn or help other people learn. Start at the lowest level of mental processing in order to build an effective and strong learning based on data as the foundation. There is no substitute for the hard work of making measurements and observations in order to collect sufficient data to develop and support a fact.

Training is focused on giving people information and facts with often insufficient data to help them understand why a fact is true. Training says, "Believe me, this is true," and maybe it is, under a certain set of circumstances or by today's standards. Perhaps if the circumstances change, the fact will no longer apply.

If the student doesn't know the data on which the fact was based, they cannot assess if the fact is still true. This is dangerous, as a "fact" then is always a fact in their mind. A cat that jumps on a hot stove will never jump on the stove again, even when it's not hot. As a consequence, the cat forever loses the opportunity to use the stove as a platform to reach some goodies on the table. Let's be careful not to take an isolated observation that "the stove is hot" and extrapolate it to a general "fact" that "stoves are always hot." Further observation would show that stoves are hot under some circumstances and not others. Don't be a cat!

Start at the bottom of the mental processing model and then climb to higher levels. Data supports the development of facts via analysis. Facts support developing knowledge by bringing together collections of facts that fit together. Knowledge supports the development of understanding by integrating many collections of facts from different areas of expertise. We form a mental model that is able to explain the outcome of situations we have observed and to predict the outcome of situations we have not yet observed. Understanding is achieved by reflection. Understanding is the level achieved by experts. We should all strive to understand our work at an expert level.

Wisdom is the accumulation of all the other levels and cannot be taught. Wisdom is the most powerful and highest level of learning. It is either learned, usually the hard way through experience and some suffering, or it is inherent in the person. It is interesting that some seven-year-olds have wisdom where some eighty-year-olds do not. I'm still trying to understand that!

> When the student is ready, the teacher appears.
> —Hindu saying

To summarize, there are many ways to learn, some better than others:

- passive (being taught or coached, reading, listening)
- active (doing, failing, analyzing, practicing)
- teaching others (delegating, coaching, mentoring)
- benchmarking (assessing and comparing ourselves to others)
- modeling (analogies, predictions, scientific method)
- reflection on past performance (reflecting on what worked and didn't work)
- mental projection to future performance and needs (preflecting)

An effective learner will use all of these ways and become a lifelong student of learning. Learn how to learn. A great way to challenge your understanding of a subject is to teach it. Good leaders teach and encourage their teams to teach each other. When we teach someone else, the process of organizing our thoughts and communicating them to another person helps us to learn the subject better ourselves. It will also highlight any holes in our understanding, and once we are aware, we can fill in by learning.

A smart man makes a mistake, learns from it, and never makes that mistake again. But a wise man finds a smart man and learns from him how to avoid the mistake altogether.
—Roy H. Williams

Persistence

For years, I've said that someday I will write a book titled *On the Third Try!* Well, how about a paragraph? No matter how simple the task, it always seems to take me two or three or more tries to accomplish something worthwhile. The fact is that persistence is a critical factor to our success as leaders. A task worth accomplishing is worth the extra effort. However, we need to consider the optimal decision point, as too much persistence or working too hard can be destructive to our teams and to ourselves.

I love the Will Rogers quote "If at first you don't succeed, try, try again." What most people don't know is that there is a second part of that quote, which is usually dropped. Will goes on to say, "And then give up. There's no sense making a damn fool of yourself." I think that just about says it all. Persistence is critical to success, up to a point, at which time you need to assess the reasons for your failure. Is the goal achievable? Are you using the right tools, the right techniques, the right resources, the right approach? Reassess the situation, adjust the goal if necessary, and then try, try again! But at some point, we need to admit failure, salvage what we can, and move on to the next challenge. Learning how to fail in a constructive manner is not a skill we ever want to use, but the fact is that we will fail occasionally in our careers, and there is value in being able to handle it well. Keeping our balance during a failure may allow us to survive to fight another day and win.

Persistence is often critical to success, but a balance must be struck and trade-offs considered. Give up too quickly, and not only will you fail often, but others will see you as weak, uncommitted, or unable to get the job done. If you are excessively persistent, you will be seen as inflexible, tyrannical, obsessed, or maybe even crazy. You have to assess the situation and the potential trade-offs. In some cases, it pays to be inflexible and persistent to the extreme. Thomas Edison and his team tried around six thousand different materials before discovering that tungsten filament could make a light bulb that operated effectively and efficiently. His perspective was not that he failed 5,999 times but rather that he successfully discovered 5,999 ways that would not work. If he had given up after 5,999 times, no one would have faulted him for a lack of persistence! However, he did not allow all these failed attempts to change his mind that an electric light bulb was possible if the right material could be found. His extreme persistence paid off.

Press on. Nothing in the world can take the place of persistence. Talent will not; nothing is more common than unsuccessful men with talent. Genius will not; unrewarded genius is almost a proverb. Education will not; the world of education is full of derelicts. Persistence and determination alone are omnipotent.
—Harry S. Truman

Success is not easy. It requires hard work and persistence. The adage "work smarter not harder" is partially right. You do want to work smart, but you still have to work hard, unless you are lucky. Grant MacDonald got it right. He said, "Successful people do *both*—they work smarter *and* harder!" Hard work can compensate for a lack of experience or skill at a task. You want to exert extra effort to learn new skills or develop a better method for solving a problem so that next time it can go much smoother and you won't have to work so hard on this task. That will free you up to spend your extra effort on learning another new task, and so on. This is how you develop yourself as a person and create a career for yourself. Some people call this activity "sharpening the saw." When cutting wood, you have to occasionally take time to sharpen the saw. Otherwise, the saw gets dull, and the work gets harder and the progress slower. Sharpening the saw is a good investment of time. If you are not building your skills and doing your job better today than yesterday, then your productivity will flatline or decline, and you will get stale, bored, and eventually eliminated.

The demands of work are getting greater and more complicated. We are expected to work safely, within company guidelines, in compliance with government regulations, according to customers' requirements, in compliance with environmental requirements, and so on. Did I mention cost requirements? It always seems to be one more thing! How can we keep up with all these demands and still get our work done? If you look at these requirements as "one more thing" to do, you will have a problem. If you prioritize or balance your efforts to manage these requirements, you will frustrate yourself and fail. You must get them all done all the time. The only way to look at these requirements is to say, "This is not one more thing; this is how we work." The important element here is to understand not just what is expected but to understand why we must work safely, as an example. If people understand what is expected of them, why it is expected, and their role in the delivery of the expectation, they can incorporate the expectation into their routine. Then it becomes part of the way they work, as opposed to being one more thing that they must do in their busy day.

There is good stress, called eustress, and bad stress, called distress. Sometimes the difference is due to our attitude, a matter of *want to* versus *have to*. Work that we enjoy or believe in, can be energizing. Work that appears, to us, to have no benefit can be draining. The number of hours worked might not matter so much if the work is good and the stress is eustress that energizes us. Feeling sorry for yourself is a sure sign that your attitude is bad and that you are experiencing distress and an energy drain. Turn this around by looking for the value that your work creates. If your work is not adding value, you shouldn't be doing it. We usually can manage our work to a greater extent than we think we can. Feeling like we are able to manage our work is the first step to changing our attitudes and changing distress into eustress. Feeling like we have no control creates frustration and can lead to feelings of hopelessness and depression. Keep an eye on your direct reports as well to make sure they are experiencing eustress and not distress.

Assess the balance between the quality of the time you spend versus the quantity. If you are finding ways to work smarter, chances are you can keep up with the increasing demands and speed that are required today. If not, then it's likely that you are on a collision course, working harder or longer or both to keep up with increasing demands and speed. Persistence is a virtue, in balance. At some point, you will get tired and your output will spiral down as your hours spiral up.

The older I get, the more I appreciate the value of good work and of having good work to do. One of the most positive statements we can make about work is that "We have work to do." It will be a bad day when you have no work to do. We need a purpose and need to add value in order to feel valued. As the leader, you must remind your teams about the value of their work. The organization's mission, vision, and values can help you to do this. Framing today's tasks in terms of our mission, vision, and values allows people to appreciate the value of their work. The value is bigger than they are. They are contributing to a meaningful achievement that leads to achieving our vision. That is powerful stuff and can help a team persist through setbacks and challenges that might otherwise result in burnout or failure.

A few years ago, I visited the cathedral in Cologne, Germany. It is a magnificent and massive structure of solid stone. The local populace started to build the cathedral in the first century of the second millennium, around AD 1100. It was not finished until around 1850. Can you imagine starting a project that you knew would not be completed by the time of your great-great-great-grandchild? Now that is a long-reaching vision and goal that motivated people to work persistently for many generations.

We want to do everything we can to prevent failure and persist in spite of the challenges, but unfortunately, failure will happen. It is a real skill to deal with failure in a positive and balanced manner. When failure happens, we want to survive the event and hopefully leverage it for future improvement. When you first become aware of an impending failure, assess your options and be candid about the situation. What can be rescued or salvaged? What is the worst that can happen? Can the worst be averted and a better outcome achieved? Do not defend or deny the situation. It is what it is. Communicate openly and completely about what has happened and what is going to happen next. Your honesty, transparency, and lack of defensiveness will win the support of others and blunt their criticism. However, don't expect to get away unscathed. You will suffer criticism for a failure. But handling a failure in a positive manner can minimize the damage to your reputation and help you to fight another day. That is your goal. Minimize the damage, maximize the learning, and position yourself for a win in the next battle. Failure can be a galvanizing event for a career or for an organization. No one wants to fail or likes to fail. But failure will happen to you in your career. How you handle it and how much you are able to learn from the failure can make the difference between a career-ending failure and a career-changing failure.

> Failure is the foundation of success; success
> is the lurking-place of failure.
> —Lao Tzu (600–550 BC)

Optimism

A companion of persistence is optimism. An important role of the leader is to provide a healthy dose of optimism and hope to his or her people. Assess the situation to strike the right balance between what is healthy and what is harmful. Employees can get tired or overwhelmed by the daily grind, and a great leader will help them see past the current issues to a future goal that is worth the hard work and persistence. The leader can provide a combination of cheerleading and support in balance with an appropriate dose of reality. A little "Ra-ra—we can do it" if presented in a humorous manner can be helpful in getting people through a difficult day. Support your people by listening to their problems and empathizing. You don't have to agree, and you certainly don't want to take away the ownership from them. Listen to their concerns and problems and allow them to do some healthy venting. Couple your listening with some encouragement to build their confidence and reenergize them.

Sometimes people misinterpret a directive from the boss and attempt to do too much. Sometimes the boss doesn't appreciate the amount of work required to accomplish a requested task and unknowingly asks for more than is reasonable. Maybe I think it should take ten minutes to perform a task, when in reality it will take two hours. Maybe if I knew it would take two hours, either I wouldn't ask for it or I would change my request to simplify it. Either way, it is important for the leader to ask questions to better understand what the employee is experiencing, then listen and, if appropriate, offer a helpful suggestion or reframe the situation in a way that makes success possible. Help the person find the hope of success in what appears to them to be an intractable situation. Help your people succeed and do not allow them to fail.

Fred: Boss, this list of jobs you asked us to get done is killing me. (It is a rare employee who will tell you this.)
Me: Really? How many items are on the list now?
Fred: There are over one hundred tasks now!
Me: Wow. That is a lot (empathy).
Fred: If I cancel all my other work, maybe I can get 80 percent of it done in two weeks. But to do that, I have to defer all preventative tasks, and that could severely impact our performance.
Me: I know I said we have to get those jobs done if we want to improve. Realistically, how many can you commit to each week and not jeopardize the regular preventative program?

Fred: I can get twenty done each week and keep up with our normal preventative tasks.

Me: Good. Plan on getting twenty done each week. I'll work with the team to go through the list to remove any jobs that can wait so you're focusing on the most urgent.

Fred: I can do that!

I gave Fred an opportunity to vent, and I listened. I gave Fred the opportunity to set his own challenge level. He clearly knows better than I do what he can commit to. There is a chance he could be lowballing me, and I could push for more, but I want to show Fred that I trust him and rely on his good judgment. The result is that Fred now has a plan that he has committed to and he can manage. Is the problem solved? Not yet, as the system we use to identify and prioritize jobs for maintenance is still not as efficient as it needs to be. But Fred now has a plan that he can handle successfully. We all get to fight another day, and after a few weeks, the job list will shrink and be manageable, with reasonable effort. People need to be successful. Nothing destroys motivation faster than feeling overwhelmed, knowing that you cannot succeed in spite of your best efforts.

Optimism and hope can be overdone, of course. Hysterical exuberance or blind optimism can be destructive in the long run. But nothing helps people through the rough spots like a little hope. The vision that the leader projects is a powerful bridge to a future state that makes today's issues and challenges worth the effort. People live on hope. Take away their hope, and the result is despair and complacency. Hope drives action. Give me hope!

Work-Life Balance

A significant challenge to maintaining persistence and optimism today is the balancing of work and personal life. Being connected every minute, to work and friends, has its benefits but also takes a toll. When balancing work and personal life demands, it is important for a leader to consider balance in their own life and in the lives of the people on their team. Hard work and persistence are critical in order to be successful. However, we also need to take care of ourselves every day and not wait for the weekend or a vacation to recuperate. This requires that we consider and maintain a healthy work-life balance every day. We need and deserve to have a personal life. "All work and no play makes Jack a dull boy" is an old saying that is too true. We need time to recharge our batteries every day in order to keep ourselves okay mentally and physically. The quality of our work will improve, and we may actually get more done if we take a break from the work. Take a break when you need it, then get back to work refreshed and energized.

I cannot work sixteen-hour days every day or cut short my sleep time and expect to be at my peak performance. Know your own body and know how much sleep you need to be well rested. Some of us need eight hours, and others can do fine on four. I need my seven hours and try my best to get it every night. There are times when that is just not possible, and I deal with it, but there is a cost. Having a routine helps tremendously. Getting to bed and rising at roughly the same time every day allows your body to get accustomed to the routine, making it easier for you to maintain. I find that sleeping late on weekends actually makes it more difficult for me on Monday morning. For me, it works better to get up at the same time on weekends and take a nap in the afternoon. We need to set some limits beyond which we will not go. There are some nonnegotiable issues like personal hygiene, a minimum amount of sleep, a minimum number of breaks, eating meals, exercising, reading, communicating with coworkers and family, and so on. Take responsibility for keeping yourself okay every day, as no one else can do it for you. Watch your team members for problems with their work-life balance, like excessive yawning, nodding off at meetings, or a change in their mood. Are they working too many hours? Are they having fun, or are they miserable and making life miserable for others too?

I once went through a particularly stressful period and started to notice a change in my stamina and health. I knew the problem was stress (distress), but what could I do? I was working on a big and important project that required a lot of my time and energy. There was no time for exercise or rest. I read a few books on the subject, and they basically all said the same thing: you need to exercise. I was shocked. How was I supposed to come home after a long, stressful, exhausting day and exercise? It seemed counterintuitive and just wrong. Well, they were right! Exercise not only keeps our bodies fit but also affects our attitude and feeling of well-being. The older I get, the more I find I need exercise. I find that even a few minutes a day helps. Know your own body and experiment with different exercises until you find what you like, what makes you feel better and doesn't hurt you. You don't need special equipment or a gym. You can jump rope without a rope; this way you never trip over the rope! Simple stretches, calisthenics, yoga, and tai chi are effective if done right as part of a daily routine. Build some moves into your daily routine so it becomes part of what you do every day. Stretch while in the shower. Do leg kicks while brushing your teeth. You can even find a minute at work to do a few push-ups!

As you consider your ideal work-life balance, examine your motivation. Do you live to work, or work to live? Work, after all, is a four-letter word. Our work defines who we are. The feeling of accomplishment we get from work is critical to our well-being. Work is getting more and more competitive every year. The pace continues to quicken every year. Timesaving and laborsaving devices seem to have the opposite impact on our lives; they enable us to do more in less time, so we do more and more in the same time. I used to think that there must be a limit to how much faster the pace can get at work and that at some point it will level off. I no longer believe that. The pace will continue to increase, and our challenge is to keep up with the new tools and new processes that allow us to do more in less time.

Don't be afraid to delegate. The goal is to get the job done well. Who does the work or how it gets done is often of less importance. Sharing the load helps to build team relationships and can be positive. Of course, if everyone else is as busy as you are, no one is likely to jump to help if you attempt to shed some of your load onto them. However, if you find a way to work together where you help them and they help you, perhaps the synergy of working together can benefit everyone. Finally, there comes a point when you simply must get help. Hiring a temporary worker for a few days to do some of your routine tasks may be an option.

Never be afraid to ask for help when you are finding it difficult to balance work and life requirements. Asking for help is not a sign of weakness; it is a sign of maturity. You have a job to do and may realize that you don't have some important element that you need for success. You can keep quiet and hope someone sees your plight and comes to your rescue before you fail. You can work twice as hard to find the missing element on your own and be a hero, assuming you succeed. You can ask someone who has the missing element for their help and get the answer quickly and efficiently. Asking for help is easier, faster, and more likely to result in success. In addition, most people are happy to help. When you ask me for help, you are telling me that you appreciate my experience and knowledge. I am flattered and willing to share. More often than not, when I ask for help, I get more than I expected. If someone turns down your request for help because they are too busy or can't be bothered, then you simply have asked the wrong person. Look for someone else. Or maybe you are not asking in the right way. "John, would you please help me with a problem I am having?" or "Can I please have a minute of your time?" Asking for help like this should do the trick.

When I am asked for help, I almost always say yes. I may not be able to drop what I am doing now, so they may have to wait a bit. However, I will help as best I can, as quickly as I can and as cheerfully as I can. I usually don't ask for any reward for my largesse. A simple thank-you is quite adequate. Responding to requests in this manner helps to create for yourself a network of colleagues who value you for your expertise and knowledge, and to whom you can go when you need help. I don't know everything and don't ever want to. However, I often know who does know what I need when I need it. I share my network with others whenever I can. The network keeps growing and getting more powerful every day, just by asking and giving help.

When you ask for help, the other person needs to see that there is going to be a benefit from their effort. My friend and counselor John Owusu told a story from his native Ghana about two men looking at a fruit tree. One asks the other for a boost up into the tree to gather some of the fruit. His friend first looks up into the tree to see if there is any fruit. He may say, "There is fruit in this tree. I will help you." But if there is no fruit in the tree, he will likely say, "There is no fruit in this tree. I will not help you." If someone refuses to help you, maybe it is because they cannot see the fruit in your tree.

If no one can help you, or you cannot delegate the task, then you may have to dig deep and get it done. Take a minute to plan your work, and if some tasks can be delayed, do so. Sometimes the stress of a short deadline and too much work will force you to find a better way. Look for it.

Balancing work and life requirements would be easier if we had more time, but time is the one thing that we all get the same amount of. It is the only truly level playing field. We cannot buy or negotiate more time. Every day has twenty-four hours for all of us. The difference is how we use our time. What do you do with your time? Make a list. Working, eating, sleeping, resting, playing, socializing, networking, reading, listening to music, learning, cleaning, practicing piano, anything else? How much time do you devote to each of these? Are you devoting the right balance of time to each activity? Chances are you are devoting too much time to work, too little time to sleep, much too little time to learning, eating too fast, and so on. Think about it and consider if your current allocation of time is going to get you where you want to get. Consider your mission and vision and whether you are going to accomplish them with the time you are allocating. A big part of the problem is that in our daily lives, the urgent tasks drive out the important tasks. We pay attention to the urgent tasks that must get done—and we get them done. When we are done and tired, how much time is left for the important but not urgent tasks that we had intended to work on but did not—again? If we continue in this fashion, we will never get those important tasks completed. I guess those "important" tasks were never that important to us after all. Is that true?

Could've, would've, should've are destructive excuses for why we didn't do something that we wanted to or should have done, but we didn't recognize the value until it was too late.

I could have done that if only I had recognized the opportunity sooner.

I would have done that if I had the time, the money, or the will.

I should have done that, and things would have turned out better.

It is worth considering what activities give you satisfaction as you search for balance in your life and work. Most people derive satisfaction from several of the following:

Physical labor	Creating
Relaxation	Building
Eating (and cooking)	Being respected
Accomplishment	Being wanted
Contributing	Being loved
Beating the odds	Appearing smart
Winning	Looking good
Being right	Being healthy
Helping someone else	Making money
Being the best	Personal development

It's hard to achieve them all, or even many at once. There are trade-offs, costs, and of course a balance to be struck. If winning is what drives you most, then being loved could be difficult to achieve, especially by those you have to beat or use to win. I heard an FDA official give a presentation at a food safety conference once, and he said, "I've always wanted to be loved and respected, but I've learned to get by being hated and feared!" Now if helping the public get safe food gives you the most satisfaction, then you may have to accept that being loved by all will be difficult to achieve and perhaps worth the trade-off.

Which of these or other satisfiers give you the greatest satisfaction?

- Are you getting as much of that result as you would like with your current work-life balance?
- Are you striving for a satisfier that is preventing you from achieving other more positive satisfiers?
- Is there a way to get more of your most powerful satisfier and still get the job done?
- Would you consider changing your work-life balance to get more of what satisfies you most?
- Would you consider moderating your pursuit of one satisfier to allow you to get more of another, more important satisfier?
- Are you optimally satisfied with your current situation?

Those are some tough questions! Don't give up easily by saying, "I don't have control over that, so I cannot change it." In the short term, that may be true, but as you consider longer time horizons, it becomes less and less true. Maybe you are imposing an imaginary box on yourself by not looking far enough ahead.

The other perspective on satisfaction is that we strive to avoid our dis-satisfiers like physical pain, rejection, criticism, being yelled at, appearing stupid, being disliked, being physically unattractive, and so on. Most people will work hard to avoid a dis-satisfier.

In the following table 4, I have tried to identify some activities that give us satisfaction and then separate the activities into seven levels, from least to greatest, based on the quality or purity of the satisfaction we derive from these activities. I suggest that *existing* provides satisfaction but not as pure or high a level of satisfaction as *experiencing, leading,* or *teaching.* The way I have separated these activities is based on my personal values. Perhaps you would put some activities higher or lower than I did. I think it is worth pondering for a few minutes what activities give you the most satisfaction. Perhaps you will develop a better understanding of your values and what drives you. This is useful information for achieving balance in your life and in appreciating how others have chosen balance in their lives.

TABLE 4

Seven Levels of Satisfaction

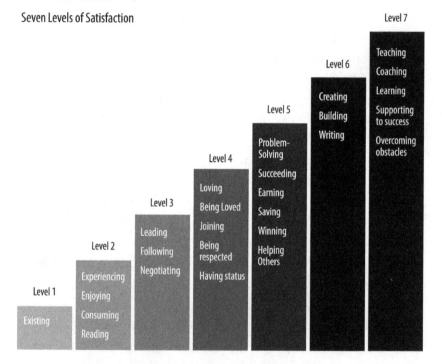

I think it is interesting to note that some projects will involve many of these activities and therefore provide satisfaction on many different levels. For example, leading a project team requires existing, experiencing, leading, following, negotiating, joining, being respected, having status, problem solving, succeeding, winning, helping others, coaching, learning, overcoming obstacles, and supporting to success. Leading a team is a powerful satisfaction driver because it involves so many satisfying activities. Consider the satisfaction we derive from being a parent; it involves almost every satisfaction driver in the chart, which may be why even though it is a long and arduous activity, so many people are motivated to be parents. Consider that it is difficult or impossible to have it all, and a reasonable balance must be sought.

We cannot have it all, but we need to at least get what is important in the time we have. One of my least favorite sayings is "I don't have time." You don't have time for what? You don't have time to do your job? You don't have time to do what is important to you? You don't have time to live your life? Nonsense. You have as much time as anyone else on this planet. You have as much time as you are going to get. It is your responsibility and challenge to allocate your precious and limited time as you see fit and as required to achieve your mission and vision. Don't shirk the responsibility of owning and controlling your time. No one else can do it for you or to you. You alone are responsible for your time. Use it well. Allocate it according to your mission, vision, and values. There will always be distracting and competing requests for your time. It is up to you to keep focused and avoid the distractions. You cannot do everything. You cannot have everything.

> You can't have everything. Where would you put it?
> —Stephen Wright

Conclusions on Leading Yourself

How can we lead others if we cannot lead ourselves effectively? It's neither easy nor trivial, but leading ourselves is critically important in that it gives others confidence in us. Developing our ability to lead and manage ourselves is a good starting point, with the end goal of being able to effectively manage others.

It all starts with having a clear understanding of your mission, vision, and values. This is the foundation on which we can build our lives and our careers. Not everyone will agree with your mission, vision, and values, but they cannot deny you the right to be yourself either. If you are the leader, they have a choice to make—align themselves with your mission, vision, and values or be forever in conflict. The best result for everyone is that people who cannot agree or align must leave and work for someone else. This is not a failure. Failure is persisting to half-heartedly support a mission that they cannot agree with.

The ability and the practice of asking questions is a useful skill for a leader to develop. Even when you know the answer—or better yet, *especially* when you know the answer—ask questions to confirm alignment and understanding. It is less confrontational than making a statement and gets people to think. It encourages openness and transparency, which are great ways to build a team. Let's find out what the team is thinking. What ideas do they have? How can we get those ideas out in the open and then support open discussion to develop and implement the good ideas? People love to contribute if they feel that it is safe to do so. If they see their ideas handled with respect and developed into winning executions, they will be highly motivated to share their ideas in the future. Virtuous cycles are the most powerful, where a small win today encourages bolder actions tomorrow. A team that is in a virtuous cycle of improvement will achieve success at a level that no one could have predicted or imagined. Be careful—this is powerful stuff!

If we are to successfully lead ourselves, we need to learn how to learn. You probably didn't learn this skill in school. The learning model used in most schools is memorizing facts at worst, and learning how to solve problems at best. Learning how to learn is an active and self-critical activity. You must challenge yourself and be willing to give up your hard-earned understanding. You must ask a lot of questions and look actively for holes in your knowledge. Building mental models is a great way to put all the pieces of the puzzle together so that you can see which pieces are missing or don't fit. However, beware, because models are simple and incomplete, and if you follow them blindly, you will ignore important data that doesn't fit with your model. This data could be exactly what you need to enhance or expand your model to improve your understanding.

Planning your activities every day based on your longer-term vision and goals is the only way to keep on track. We don't want to wake up five years from now in the same place we are today, not that where we are today is so bad, but if we don't progress, we are falling behind or stagnating. Don't be afraid to dream and use those dreams to drive your goals. Dreams give us hope and something to shoot for. Converting the dream into real, persistent actions over a period of years is how we achieve great goals. Look at anyone who has achieved a great or "impossible" goal, and you will find a dream at the base of their determined work over many years. It may have started as a dream, but it ended as a goal and a real achievement.

Optimism and pessimism in proper balance are necessary to keep us honest and motivated. Without optimism, we become miserable. Without pessimism, we become fools.

There is no substitute for working hard and persisting in the face of obstacles. Very rarely will events or activities go as originally planned. We need to persist and be prepared with backup plans. We need to ask for help when we need it and maybe even when we don't, just to exercise that option and create networks of support that will help us when we really need it. We are not islands. I like to say that I'm only a humble stick, but I'm part of a tree. That is where the real strength is.

We have to take care of ourselves. As a leader, very often no one else can take care of us, at least not at work. Keep a sharp eye on your attitude and mood. Persistence is important, but overwork can lead to destructive behaviors. Keeping work, play, and rest in the proper balance is a real challenge. Making sure that our team members do the same is also critical to success. Just keep in mind that the optimal balance for them is unique to them. What works for you may not work for them. Support them to decide for themselves how best to manage their own work-life balance.

Developing wisdom is a lifelong quest. Some of us are lucky to be born with wisdom or develop it easily. Others never develop it. A strong and supportive team can help members with wisdom come forward and give the team the guidance it needs. The others who are technically smart but not so wise must be allowed to present their best ideas for the team to evaluate and use. Balancing the skills and weaknesses of team members by appreciating the unique contributions of each is the way to build a team. Not everyone can be smart, and not everyone is wise. Take what each has to offer and combine it synergistically to bring out the best in everyone.

Integrity is table stakes. Don't even play the game if you are not willing and able to commit to integrity. Being willing to take risks for the success of the team is a sign of a mature and confident leader. You won't always win, but the wins you achieve will make it worth the price. You have to have enough conviction to state your case, especially when you are sure that you are right, and be willing to accept the fallout along with the accolades. It helps to keep your emotions under control and remain as professional as possible.

Leading yourself is not easy, but it is the first step to becoming a great leader of others. Maintaining your own balance in the face of challenges and difficulties makes it easier for you to stay on track to achieve your goals. Keep your eye on the mission and never compromise your values. There will be good days and bad days, successes and failures. Learn from the failures and celebrate the successes.

Chapter 3

Balance in Leading Others

In this chapter, we will consider some of the factors that are important in leading other people. People do not follow us just because we tell them to or even because we are their boss, although being their boss does help create that expectation. Rather, people follow a leader that they have confidence in. If you want to be a leader, and hopefully a good one, you will need to take some steps to make it happen.

Developing Others

One important aspect of being a leader is to build your team by developing their skills. People love working for a leader who helps them grow and be successful. In order to be successful in supporting each other, they need to be capable of backing each other up when the need arises. The leader must facilitate the sharing and development of skills between the team members. One way to do this is to hold formal training events where we bring in an expert. This is an excellent way to improve skills, but it is also expensive and time-consuming. Therefore, we don't do it very often or at least not often enough for optimal results. Another option is to have them learn from each other by sharing their experiences, allowing them to learn by teaching and by doing. The leader can create situations in the course of normal business activities to develop skills in their people. The benefits are low cost, with little or no extra time spent, the learning is relevant to the work situation, and since we are not waiting for a special event, we can do it often, perhaps every day. This can be an effective and fun way to build learning into our everyday work. It can be incremental, so the risk of failure is low, especially when other team members are there to watch and step in if a problem arises. This can also be a great way to build team spirit and cohesiveness. Find ways to build skill development into your daily work and don't wait for a special event.

None of us is perfect, and none of us has the perfect skill set or behaviors to do the job we are doing. Do you look at people as round pegs (skill set and behaviors) that we force into square holes (jobs)? When we look for the perfect person or expect our current people to have the perfect skill set or behaviors, we are bound to be disappointed. This creates a tough choice; we can help them succeed, we can criticize them hoping they will change and improve, or we can fire them and search for the perfect person. My suggestion is that we have a responsibility to do everything we can to help them succeed. If they fail, we have failed. It is our job to help them be successful. Now there are some people who will resist our help and fail anyway. In those cases, our decision is much easier—it's time for a change!

I had a guy working for me—let's call him Bob. Bob had a lot of good traits. He was dedicated, hardworking, and technically strong. He had a few issues as well, which were impacting his performance in a negative way. He was doing his job the way he had always done it and was failing. He was pushing his people to improve and blaming them for the failures. They were having a rough time and not having any fun. The result was that the people were demoralized and just going through the motions, so I had to make a decision. We talked, and I asked lots of questions about the work and about how Bob was interacting with his people. I found out that there were some basic technical flaws in his approach to the work. In addition, the balance of positive feedback to criticism was way off, meaning mostly negative and too little positive. I asked him if he would allow me to help him. He realized his tenuous situation and agreed to work with me. We changed the way he organized the work and the way he managed his people. We gave people ownership of specific tasks and posted a schedule of work that made it clear who was responsible for what area on each day of the week. The schedule repeated each week so that people did the same job every week. This simple change allowed them to improve and find ways to do the work better in less time. Each day when they came into work, people knew their assignments for the day and were able to go straight to work without wasting their time or their supervisor's time. Bob would follow up with them at the end of the day to review their work and give them feedback on it. He gave positive feedback on the work that was done well, and he coached his people to do better on the work that needed improvement. We asked the people to help us improve the work and get it done in less time so we could accomplish more. They responded and started taking pride and ownership in the work. For the first time in a long time, they were succeeding. Bob started to lead his team, and the team responded enthusiastically when they saw the work getting done and the improvements being made. When we had an inspection and achieved the first Superior rating that the facility had ever received in its forty-six-year history, Bob and the team could not have been prouder or happier. The improvements and good work continued, and the team's performance continued to improve along with morale. We went on to score two more Superior ratings in the next two years. Bob and his people were a different team than before. What had changed? Weren't they and Bob the same people who had been failing? Wasn't Bob the same person who I considered firing a few months before? They were the same people, but their behavior was different. They were now successful and had confidence that they could succeed. They had experienced success, and they liked it. Now I could back off and let Bob lead his reinvigorated team. They reached levels of performance and tackled new challenges that I hadn't even thought of. That is what good leadership does. It takes people to places and levels of performance that they and others had not even thought of. One more thing. Who got the credit for this turnaround in performance? Bob and his team, of course—and they deserved it.

Remember that competency develops in a vacuum. This means that as long as you or someone else is the subject matter expert (SME), people will defer to the SME and will not develop their skills. If you want people to learn and climb the learning curve, you have to take away the SME and allow them to experiment and fail. The SME can be the safety net to make sure they don't do irreparable damage to themselves or the business, but they must be allowed to fail and learn. A child will not learn to walk unless you allow them to fall.

You may have to fight with your people to get them to develop. Development is change, and most people resist change. "Why should I change? I've gotten along like this for many years." You will probably have to make them uncomfortable and maybe yourself too. You will probably have to tell them tough things that they may not want to hear. I've had this happen several times in my career, with good people who were performing their jobs well, but they weren't improving. Their performance was adequate today, but in three years or five years, if they didn't find a way to improve, they would become obsolete or inadequate. People often don't see this, because they are not looking into the future or expecting that the future will be so different from today. As their leader, you need to show them this and set expectations for them to improve.

I have to say that sometimes it didn't work the way I had hoped it would. I experienced a situation once where I had a very competent person working for me and I was pushing her to improve because I knew she could do it. Of course, I could have remained positive and avoided the challenge to improve. After all, she was performing her job well—just not as well as I knew she could. She unfortunately didn't appreciate my challenges at the time, thinking that I was being too difficult, and she left the company for another job. In hindsight, I didn't have the ratio of positive to negative right; even though I was trying to help her improve, I wasn't positive enough and she only heard the negative. As it turned out, it was a good learning experience for both of us. A year later, I met her at a meeting, and I was relieved when she told me that I had been right; she was hearing the same message from her new boss, and she appreciated that I had tried to push her to improve. We have been great friends ever since.

In another situation, I had a person working for me whose technical writing skills were weak. It would take her weeks to write a report or a procedure that I thought she should be able to write in a few hours or a few days at most. I discovered, after some observation, that the reason it took so long was that she was getting help from her friends in the office. This was okay with me; in fact, I considered it to be a sign of resourcefulness, and I applauded it. However, when we were on a trip and her friends were not there, she was unable to write a report. I explained to her that she needed to be able to write reports on her own and to do it quickly and efficiently. I challenged her on a trip, when she was alone, to write a report on the day's events and get it to me that night. She wouldn't have time to collaborate. And I wanted to know how long it took for her to write the report. She refused to do it. The next morning, there was still no report. She asked me why I was being so tough on her. I explained that either she would learn how to write a report quickly by herself or I would have to send her back to a plant operation, where she would not have to do this. But if she wanted to work in my group, this was a skill that I expected her to have, and I was willing to work with her to develop. It takes a lot of energy, fighting with people to get them to change when they don't see the need. After a few days of going back and forth, with my explaining how to write the report and her practicing doing it in a shorter time, she got it and understood now that she could do it as I expected.

How would you have handled these situations? Are you willing to say the tough things that need to be said? Do you care enough about your people to be tough on them? Do they care enough to accept when you are tough on them?

Motivation and Expectations

One of the most difficult lessons I have learned is that, as a leader, you cannot motivate another person to do anything. You can beg, plead, suggest, persuade, convince, incent, lead, cajole, push, demand, order, or coerce, but you cannot motivate. Where is the balancing sweet spot along this continuum? What is the optimal balance between begging and coercing that is going to get my beloved but stubborn employee to move toward the goal? I suggest that the balancing sweet spot we seek is to help them become self-motivated. They need to want to perform the task, and how you achieve that depends as usual on you, the situation, how much time and patience you have, the cost of failure, the other person, and the goal itself. People, if left on their own, will work to meet their own personal standards, not yours. Of course, you expect them to meet your standards, but since their standards are different, there is a conflict.

The way around this dilemma is to define what you expect them to do in terms of goals. Challenge them to share the vision and gain their interest in becoming self-motivated toward achieving the goal—now their goal. It is easier to achieve agreement on and commitment to goals rather than standards. Standards are personal; goals must be shared. People are usually unwilling to change their work standards, but goals are bigger than us, so getting agreement on a goal is much easier and less emotionally charged. Define success and explain the value of achieving it. Allow them the freedom to redefine the goal upward if they can find a better approach or achieve a greater goal. The combination of a clear goal, the reward of success, the challenge itself, the safe environment, and the freedom to be creative can be powerful motivators—much more powerful and sustaining than coercion or futile attempts to motivate.

If your direct report is not achieving the agreed-upon goals, you need to consider why. Are they capable? Do they have the necessary resources and skills? Maybe they have failed before and are afraid of failing again. A powerful way to get them to buy into the goal is to coach and provide a safe environment in which they can work and stretch their skills. Provide a safety net, and do not allow them to fail. This will build trust and self-confidence. It's a difficult lesson for a leader to learn—to trust another person with "your" goal. We want our people to be self-motivated and to feel free to perform, hopefully even to perform better than the goal. The reward for you, the leader, is greater than just achieving a goal; you have helped create a successful and self-motivated person. They will walk through walls for you. When you help a child learn how to ride a bike for the first time, the presence of your steadying hand on the bicycle gives them the confidence to pedal and learn the feel of balance, until you remove your hand and they ride away, unaware at first that they are balancing without your help.

Exceeding what is expected of us is a powerful way to show our boss and the organization that we are a serious performer. I tell my kids, "When doing a job, exceed what is expected of you, and you will create opportunity for your entire career." There are four levels of performance—fail to meet expectations, meet expectations, exceed expectations, and delight. Delight means delivering much more than was expected. Delighting your boss is a sure way to differentiate yourself from the crowd. You want to become the go-to person and consistently deliver more than was expected of you. This is what differentiates top performers from the ordinary.

A window of opportunity won't open itself.
—David Weinbaum

Shared expectations can influence an entire community to behave differently. We have all seen ghetto sections of a city, and maybe you wonder what is different about these blocks compared to different-looking blocks a half mile away. In the Bronx, there is a street called Arthur Avenue that is right in the middle of a not-so-great area. When you get to Arthur Avenue, you notice a stark and immediate change for the better. The streets are clean, there is no graffiti on the buildings, families are walking on the streets, and there are nice shops and restaurants. What changed? Why did it change?

A lot has to do with shared expectations. If the people who live on a block expect the buildings to be free from graffiti, they will find a way to do it. If they expect the street to be clean, they will find a way to keep it clean. If they expect to go to college, they probably will find a way to go. If they expect their work to be done well, they will find a way to do it well. The opposite will also be true. If they expect to be late, they will probably be late. Our expectations define who we are and what we do both as individuals and as a community. The lesson is that if you want to change performance, change the expectations. If you want to change the performance of an organization, work with the people in the organization to define and agree on the expectations. As a leader, I do not want to tell you what to do or how to do it; that is your job, and that is what I pay you to do. However, in order to be successful, we need to define and agree on the expectations. The most powerful and effective way to do that is having and communicating clear goals that are based on our shared mission, vision, and values.

Rudy Giuliani's book, *Leadership*,[7] explains how he changed the expectations in New York City by selectively enforcing the law on a few small but visible crimes to send a message that things had changed. He targeted the people who harassed drivers while stopped at a light to wash their windshields, expecting a handout. There was no law against washing car windows, so the city had never tried to stop this annoying behavior. Rudy and his police commissioner got creative and started charging them with jaywalking! This was a creative use of an existing ordinance that allowed him to set and communicate a new expectation—we won't tolerate harassment of visitors in the city. He targeted law enforcement of graffiti artists on buildings and subway cars. He convinced Walt Disney Corporation to invest in setting up a Disney store in Times Square to show everyone that expectations were changing. David Dinkins and Ed Koch had started the process of revamping Times Square years before by condemning and driving out the peep shows and adult stores that had defined Times Square for so many decades. Giuliani built on this foundation by making it clear that expectations had changed, and things did change in a big way. All types of serious crime plunged. Times Square went from the seediest part of town to a family and tourist attraction. The city started on a virtuous cycle of investment and improvement from one end to the other. Who could have expected that?

Destructive Doubt versus the Power of Dare

Once we have agreed upon the shared goals with our team, it is important that we dare and support them to success while avoiding discouraging them with doubts. We unintentionally undermine the initiative and motivation of our people by doubting them, perhaps unintentionally. We say something like "I need a plan from you on how to restructure your team to improve performance" or "Prepare a presentation on how you can improve the performance of your team." These imply that performance is not up to expectations now and needs to be improved. I'm saying that I have doubts about how you are handling the situation. Perhaps I am unaware of or unsatisfied with the changes that you have already made to improve team performance. This is a lot of negative baggage that I've just dumped on my direct report. If I don't explain what I mean, they will wonder what it is that I have doubts about, and their imagination will run wild in a negative direction. This is not what I intended. Now I have to do damage control and bring them back to a positive frame of mind. It will make life for all a lot easier and more pleasant if we can avoid going to the negative in the first place.

The other problem with expressing doubts is that I don't give the other person any context or goal to help them understand what I expect them to do. They have to guess what I mean by "improve." Do I mean that I want them to reduce head count? Do I mean that I want them to reduce cost? Do I mean that I want them to increase output or quality? I could mean many things by "improve." My direct report may go off and work on improving throughput by speeding up the line by 10 percent. This could be a significant achievement or a meaningless one if, for example, the line is not running at capacity now and paid hours are fixed by a contract.

A more positive way is to dare our team with a suitable, well-defined stretch goal. "Is there a way to restructure to increase output per man-hour by 10 percent?" "What can we do to reduce unplanned downtime by 20 percent?" "I challenge you and your group to find a way to increase output per shift by 20 percent to meet the needs of the Smith project." The stretch goal does not doubt or imply anything negative about past or current performance, while instigating creative restructuring of existing resources to achieve a positive and well-defined goal. My direct report has a much clearer picture of what I am asking them to do. We are already one step closer to success. One approach creates destructive confusion; the other defines a goal worth achieving. Dare your people to succeed, and do not doubt!

Rewards and Recognition

Rewards and recognition are important in incenting people to do what we need for them to do. Rewards are giving people something of value, such as cash, a gift card, a pen, a TV, or some other valuable item. Recognition, on the other hand, can be a pat on the back, a handshake, a thank-you, a note to their file, an employee-of-the-month award, a plaque, and so on.

With rewards and recognition, like everything else, there is an optimal balance. Too little reward or recognition can make people feel unappreciated. Too much makes them feel entitled to the reward, even when their performance is not so great. Balance is important, and it varies by person. Some people shy away from any kind of recognition or are embarrassed when recognized, sometimes resulting in poorer performance. Other people thrive on recognition and will not perform without it. With adequate recognition, these people can become star performers. It is critical to know your people and what makes each of them tick.

Recognition can cost nothing. Often, the most effective recognition is just a thoughtful word or a pat on the back. Context is the key. Make sure to recognize people for their behavior or performance, not for who they are. If the recognition is not specific enough, it can be confusing, so make sure it is clear for what behavior or performance they are being recognized. Recognizing a good performance or behavior is a powerful way to reinforce the good behavior or performance so that it occurs more often in the future. Recognizing the same behavior or performance more than once can be demotivating to people, as they think you forgot and therefore you really don't care. Combining challenge and recognition makes the recognition even more powerful. "I'm impressed that you now consistently perform that equipment changeover in ten minutes. Do you think it's possible to do even better?" When they improve to eight minutes, *you must* recognize them, or you have lost the ability to reinforce the improvement and they will go back to ten minutes or worse for sure.

Rewards are completely different from recognition. Rewards cost money and have a different effect on people. Rewards can be even more powerful than recognition in reinforcing or incenting behavior or performance. After all, we are working for the money ultimately. "Show me the money" is a perfectly reasonable attitude when real performance improvements are desired and delivered. Recognition may not be enough. However, there is a real risk with rewards that after a few rounds of rewards, people will feel entitled to the reward and the reward is no longer rewarding. Rewards can be a drug to which people become addicted, requiring ever-higher levels of rewards to have any impact on performance. A great book on the subject is *Punished by Rewards* by Alfie Kohn.[8] It is best to use rewards sparingly, intermittently, or not at all so that people do not become hooked on the reward. Remember that the ultimate reward is success. It is better to drive performance with a mission, vision, and values. Focus people on achieving and celebrating success, rather than the monetary reward. However, if success delivers real dollars, then sharing some with the people may be appropriate and beneficial.

Ownership

Getting our people to want to achieve a shared goal requires a balance between ownership and accountability. Ownership represents a deep level of personal, positive interest in the achievement of a task. Accountability implies a motivation to achieve in order to avoid a negative consequence. How we balance ownership and accountability will determine the balance of negative and positive motivation driving our team. Are we driving toward the positive, avoiding a negative, or striking an effective balance of both? Creating a sense of ownership is the most positive way to lead ourselves and others to become self-motivated and self-rewarded to achieve a task. When people own something, they care for it much more deeply than if they are only caretakers who will be held accountable. They own not only the task but also the result. If the result is not up to our agreed standard, they will find a way to compensate. They will not make excuses or blame the circumstances or other team members as they might if they were merely caretakers. As owners, they care about the result, the other team members, the techniques used, and so on. They care about and take personal interest in the result. When people are held accountable to do something, they work only enough to avoid punishment. They will rarely go beyond what is expected. They say things like "I'm not being paid to do that" or "That's not *my* job." If the result is not up to our agreed standard, they may balk and blame someone else in order to avoid being held accountable.

When people take personal ownership, the leader must be willing to give up some control by transferring part of the ownership and responsibility. When there is a clear definition of roles and responsibilities, creating personal ownership is transformational and powerful. Clear goals, expectations, and definition of roles can allow all team members to own a piece of the task without conflict.

How do we get others to own a task? It could be as simple as asking them. As the leader, when we communicate with a vision, a strategy based on the vision, and the tactical tasks needed, we have great power in asking others for their ownership of those tasks. Our team members will understand how important it is for them to get the task done properly, in support of the vision and strategy. "John, I appreciate that this is a difficult task that will challenge your skills. I need you to take ownership and see it through to completion. Can you form a team and get this done?" The answer will rarely be no, and if it is no, it will be because John really believes that he cannot get the job done and cares enough to say so. That is ownership too.

I've seen email chains involving dozens of people that bounce around for a month. The initiator is looking for an answer to a question, and no one knows the answer. Each person in turn forwards it to another person in another department who they think may have the answer. This is a waste of time based on a failure to take ownership, with the result that the question goes unanswered and the organization fails. Is it that people don't care? I doubt it. Is it because no one has the answer? Yes, that is true, but it's deeper than that. The bottom line is that no one was willing to say, "I will take ownership of this and get you an answer." Once someone takes ownership, they will scout around to find a person who has the answer. This requires persistence and resourcefulness—characteristics displayed by an owner. Someone must take ownership!

Ideas

Leading others successfully requires the effective generation and nurturing of ideas. The balance is in how we support the generation, expression, sharing, development, and implementation of ideas. Supporting every idea can cause chaos, while failing to support the process will stifle creativity. Ideas drive innovation, and innovation drives growth. However, ideas are a dime a dozen. Good ideas are worth a little more than that, but the point is that an idea is not worth much unless it is supported and executed. As a leader, we want to create an environment where people feel free to express their ideas, share their ideas with team members, and build on each other's ideas. We want to encourage respect for ideas, even when the idea may be a bit crazy. In fact, crazy ideas may be the best of all. Crazy ideas can be fun and can spark a creative and feasible idea that can then be implemented. Keep the group focused on developing a good idea, not a perfect idea, and then define some steps to test it.

> There is nothing more powerful than
> an idea whose time has come.
> —Victor Hugo

Execution of ideas can be risky, especially if it is a new, untried idea. Some companies identify one branch office as a test laboratory where ideas can be tried at low cost and low risk. Walmart uses its vast and almost instantaneous IT system to track sales of individual items in stores across the country in real time. A manager in Bentonville can see that unit sales of fizzy water are higher recently in the Boise store than anywhere else the product is for sale. They can contact the department manager in Boise and ask what they did. The manager in Boise sends a picture of the display he set up that is generating the extra sales. The manager in Bentonville sends the picture and a request to all Walmart stores to execute the same display. Within hours, a good idea is identified and replicated in thousands of stores across the country, and sales of fizzy water can benefit everywhere. It is a very powerful system. A good idea was generated, identified, and replicated quickly and efficiently. The manager in Boise feels like a genius and is forever motivated to be creative. The entire organization sees what happened, and people say, "I can do that too," and they do.

If a chicken is just an egg's way of making another egg, then a company might be considered just an idea's way of making another idea. It's not the company that's important, it's the people and the ideas in it that must move forward and reproduce.
—Russel Howard, CEO of Maxygen in Richard Dawkins's book *The Selfish Gene*

Ideas are fragile, and sometimes they require a lot of nurturing and protection, or they can be damaged beyond repair by those who can see only the potential negative aspects. An idea is a kernel, a seed, an embryo. It is not fully formed or fully thought out. It takes a lot of work to convert an idea into a successful execution.

The positive points must be developed, and the negative points either mitigated or eliminated. Too many good ideas fail to reach execution because of early critical reviews that put too much emphasis on the negative aspects and not enough on the positives. Every idea needs a champion—a leader—who takes ownership of the idea and then works hard to direct the work to transform the undeveloped potential in the idea into a winning execution. Thomas Edison did not come up with the idea for the light bulb. He recognized the potential in the idea and found a way to overcome the negatives that had confounded other people. It took huge persistence to do so. It was his conviction that the potential benefit of the idea was great and worth the investment of time and effort to develop it. Are you the champion of ideas or the gladiator who cuts them up in pieces to kill them? Are you a gardener who nurtures or a warrior who kills ideas that are not ready for execution? A game-changing idea, properly nurtured and developed to execution, will do just that—change the game for you and your competitors.

> An invasion of armies can be resisted, but
> not an idea whose time has come.
> —Victor Hugo

The risk of missing a good idea by killing it too soon is that you miss out on the opportunity and your competitor may find it, both to your serious detriment. We need both the champion and the warrior roles in the proper balance. To do this effectively, we need to assess the idea critically in order to identify the good, bad, and unknown elements. Consider if you have adequately thought about and assessed the idea. Do you understand the potential benefits and pitfalls? Have you looked for ways to compensate for or eliminate the negatives while building on the positives? Here is a test I use to tell me the answer to these questions. I ask a few questions about the negatives and the positives. If I can get the other person to "I don't know" or "Gee, I haven't looked into that" in three questions or less, then I know they haven't really considered the idea, at best, or they don't know what they are talking about, at worst. Either way, they are the wrong person to be entrusted with the idea, or I need to do a better job of leading them to be the champion that this idea deserves.

> The difficulty lies not so much in developing
> new ideas, as in escaping from old ones.
> —John Maynard Keynes

Another hint that they may be the wrong person to champion the idea is if they focus all their attention on what is wrong with the idea and why it won't or can't possibly work, and too little or no attention on what is right with it. Then I know they are not a champion; they are an idea killer. I need to find a champion or transform them into a champion. Now of course, even with a dedicated and committed champion, some ideas are just not ready for execution. We have to be careful not to invest too much time or resources into a potentially good idea that will require more resources than we can afford. We must balance effort, commitment, and resources with current needs so that we do not lose what we have. A bird in hand is indeed worth two in the bush!

Accountability

Accountability is the opposing attribute to ownership. Likewise, it is an important behavior of effective leadership and a difficult one to properly balance. Too little accountability can result in anarchy and licentiousness in the workplace. Too much accountability can cause needless anxiety and stress. The right level of accountability creates clarity about who owns a specific task, what results are expected of them, and when they are expected to deliver. Coordination between people and groups becomes easier when everyone knows when a task will be completed by one person or group and passed on to the next. Anxiety and tension are low; productivity and morale are high. This is the balance of accountability we want to achieve.

The most important part of holding ourselves or others accountable is establishing clear expectations. Accountability without clear expectations can be especially destructive. "Thanks for sending me this report today as we agreed. Did I mention that it needs to be in Arial font and double-spaced? No? Sorry, you need to redo it." Rework due to failure to communicate expectations creates frustration and anxiety. I planned and did the job according to the communicated expectations, and where there were no stated expectations, I worked to my own expectations. Now you tell me that the result is unacceptable and must be redone to meet an expectation you forgot to express? This is disruptive and frankly offensive, as you are telling me that my judgment is wrong. Make sure the expectations are clear. And if you don't set an expectation on some attribute, be prepared to accept some creativity. If you didn't say it must be in Arial font and they deliver it in Cambria, then you should be flexible and accept it in Cambria.

Sometimes people will insert their creativity into a project and violate, or in their mind exceed, the stated expectations. You need to weigh the cost of asking them to redo the work according to the stated expectation or, worse, an unstated expectation. It will be deflating and demotivating, but if the expectation was clear and is important, then perhaps it will be a worthwhile lesson. To be fair to both sides, expectations need to be clearly stated and important to the project. If an expectation really doesn't matter, then why make it an expectation? And if it really is important, then it should have been clearly stated and agreed to before the work started so that accountability is possible. How will you handle a situation where the team has been creative in a way that violates and maybe exceeds the stated expectations? How you handle this situation will send a powerful message for future projects. Letting it slide this time tells the team that it's okay to ignore the expectations next time, when in their judgment they are able to deliver beyond the expectations. Being inflexible and demanding that the expectations are met, regardless of a possible improvement, tells the team that it is not okay in the future to violate the expectations, even if they are able to deliver what may be a better result. Sometimes "better" is better, and sometimes not, but be aware of the message you are sending.

As a leader, effective accountability requires that you step back to get adequate perspective so you can assess if progress is being made. Progress can be slow, and you don't want to be overly impatient or you could kill the initiative. On the other hand, regress can also be slow, making it difficult to detect whether the operation is improving or worsening. Make sure that the key performance indicators (KPIs) that you watch are accurate and meaningful to measure what matters in your operation. Read Malcolm Gladwell's book *The Tipping Point*[9] to see how small improvements can tip a situation and result in large changes. To make progress, put one foot in front of the other. If you do this, you will get to your destination. Is your progress aligned with your mission, vision, and values? Are people cooperating and coordinating their efforts in support of the vision? If so, then even small progress can be a sign that the ship is turning, and bigger, faster progress will come soon.

People who are good at accountability do so in a low-key but consistent manner. Sometimes people forget a deadline, so a gentle reminder about the memo that was promised to you today can actually be helpful if done in a low-key manner. I like to say in a joking way, "I can't wait to see your report!" They get the message and appreciate that I care enough to help them be successful and avoid failure. Being authoritative and heavy-handed can be destructive but may be necessary to send a message to a chronic underachiever. In order to keep anxiety low and productivity high, you need to be consistent in how you apply accountability. You can be a stickler for detail if you have clearly communicated that expectation and all are held consistently accountable. You have probably heard people say, "He is tough but fair," in describing a boss that they liked. Clearly communicating the goal is necessary, as is being a competent, authentic leader.

Paying Attention

People love being recognized by the leader. The simple act of saying hello or good morning can be a powerful and positive experience. The effect is especially dramatic when we consider the alternative, which is you walking right past them without making eye contact or acknowledging their presence or existence. They may wonder, *What's wrong?* or *What did I do wrong?* Of course, you have given them no basis for feeling like they did something wrong or that there is anything wrong, unless they have a guilty conscience. However, in the absence of information, people imagine the worst. When they see the boss with their head down and not acknowledging people as they walk around, they think something is wrong—perhaps with them. So, keep your head up (even when something is wrong!) and acknowledge the people you pass as you walk around. If you know their name, use it. If you know something about them personally, use it discretely. "Morning, Joe. See that game last night?" "Morning, Sue. How did your son do in the playoff yesterday?" "Morning,

Sally. Thanks for keeping your work area clean. Looks great!"
"Morning, Susan. Nice socks (bright pink)!"

A leader can lift the mood of the whole office by walking around and recognizing people by name and being upbeat. You can have the opposite effect by skulking around with your troubles on your brow. Do you know what word people love to hear the most and never get tired of hearing from their boss? It is their name. Their name is sweet music when said by the boss. When the boss simply says my name, I perk up and listen. When they use my name in a cheery salutary greeting, I am energized. It costs nothing to recognize a person by name, and it tells them "I know you, and you are important to me." Adding a short personal message, no matter how trite, tells them "I know you as a person, and I care about you."

I was the new plant manager, and after a few months, a few people came up to me and said, "You're different from the plant managers we've had in the past."

I asked, "How is that?"

They said, "You know my name." This was important to them. How much effort did it take on my part? People love to hear their name and love to be recognized by the boss. Do it often.

When I first started at a new company, I was shocked to see the president walk around the plant every week in his pin-striped suit and go out of his way to say hello to every employee. He walked up and said something to each one. The reaction was a smile or a laugh. I don't know what he said to them, but he got a similar reaction from each person as he went around. It was like an old friend had dropped into town and stopped by to say hello. The positive feeling he created in the team was incredible. I make a point of doing the same when I come into an office or plant. I am naturally an introvert and have to work hard to behave like an extrovert, but it is worth the effort. The better you know people, the easier it is to talk to them. If you don't know them, ask them a question. Invariably, you will learn something that can be the spark for conversation the next time you walk by. Then in the future, when you need to talk to them about a challenge or an issue in their performance, it will be a lot easier for you to do so.

Talk to all the people, not just your peers and superiors. A leader can have a positive impact when they recognize anyone in the organization, but the impact is especially powerful when you recognize the people who are below you on the organization chart. These are the people who do the grunt work. They often feel unappreciated or undervalued, and the work they do is critical to the company. See what happens if you run the office without a cleaning crew for a week and how the quality of life deteriorates. Recognizing people and knowing their names is a powerful way for the leader to say, "I know who you are, and I value your contribution to our company." Did you realize that when you said, "Good morning, Joe," you were saying all that?

I have known bosses who can drop the temperature in a room by thirty degrees just by walking in. We used to joke about their ability to do this through just their demeanor and body language. They walk stiffly, look at no one, avoid eye contact, say nothing, and make believe they are the only person in the room. Now maybe they think this is the best way to avoid interrupting the group, but actually this is the most disruptive. Other bosses walk into the room, smile at the people there, acknowledge them with a sweep of eye contact and maybe just a wave or a quick hello, and quickly integrate themselves into the meeting. The temperature in the room doesn't change, and the mood of the team improves. The boss is here.

When you visit a new office or meet new people in the office, introduce yourself and ask them their name and where they work.

Drop the formality of titles. "Hello. I'm Len. I'm here to work on the Smith project. What's your name?" "Hi. I'm Len. I work in Quality. Welcome to the organization." Talk to them about what they do. Tell them what you are doing and ask them to help you with your work. People love to help when asked nicely. Remembering the name of a receptionist and saying, "Hello, Jeanne. I'm Len Heflich from ABC here to meet with the Smith project team. Can you please point me toward the coffee and the conference room?" is a great way to break the ice and get Jeanne to be an ally.

Say please and thank you. Sure, you're the boss, and you don't have to say please when you want something done. People are just doing their jobs. True—and saying please and thank you really does help. It is the little extra stuff you do as the leader that can make a big difference in people's attitude and performance. As the leader, you can influence the mood of your team by your behavior. If you act like things are good, they will get better. If you act like things are bad, they will get worse. Set the mood by your behavior.

Paying attention to people means making yourself accessible when they need you. An open-door policy is good, but you really must keep the door open and make people feel welcome to come in. When I was plant manager, I maintained an open door not only in that the physical door was open, but I invited people to come into my office, and then I made them feel welcome. I paid attention to them. After a few minutes, it became obvious to me that several of the people who came into my office had never been in the plant manager's office before, and these were people who had worked in that plant for over twenty years! What do you think this did for their morale? How do you think this affected their behavior when a few weeks later I had to ask them to support an unpopular but necessary restructure?

Sometimes people just need an opportunity to vent. They may not like some change or policy that impacts them. They may realize that it cannot be changed and may even be willing to accept it. Allowing them to vent their frustration or concerns and paying attention to them can be constructive. Sometimes that is all they want—just someone to listen to them and acknowledge their concern. In cases like this, I don't try to sell them on the change. They have heard all that before from me and others. They realize that the change is coming. Just allowing them to vent and listening to them is therapeutic and allows a good worker to clear their conscience and get back to work. Paying attention to people is a powerful way to recognize them.

Difficult People

Maintaining our balance when dealing with people we find difficult is a special challenge. We cannot make everyone happy. We need to deal effectively with superiors, peers, and subordinates while expecting each to react differently to us, as their agenda will differ from others' and from ours. We already discussed the difficulty of motivating someone who is on our team. How much more difficult will it be to motivate or coordinate activities with a peer or superior? The most difficult role of a leader is getting peers and superiors to support our efforts.

We will find that there are some people with whom we can establish a positive rapport in minutes. We are almost instantly on the same wavelength. We are able to relate and find common ground between us. These people become our friends and allies. We may have the opposite experience with some other people. For some reason, we cannot get along. We misunderstand or misinterpret every word that the other says, and we imagine the other is doing all sorts of terrible things. For some unknown reason, we think the other is a bad person. Maybe we or they are not entirely imagining, meaning there is a kernel of truth to our feelings, but we or they or both of us are likely blowing the situation out of proportion. Perhaps we have unknowingly offended them in the past. We forgot or didn't notice the offense, but of course they noticed and remembered. These people become our enemies or rivals in the organization. Maybe there is jealousy between us because of our or their success or position. We cannot find a way to trust these people, and we cannot understand their motivation no matter how hard we try. I have been in situations like this and could not figure it out either. For some reason, our relationship with these people is strained at best, outright hostile at worst, and not predictable.

My experience is that out of a hundred people, there will be one person with whom I cannot get along, no matter how hard I try. One in a hundred may be manageable and may be a good indication that my behavior is okay with most people. What if the ratio is one out of ten? Or five in ten? A higher ratio of people with whom we cannot get along may indicate that we are the problem. The point is you will never get along with everyone, and depending on the balance you strike in your behavior, you will get along with more or less people. How many people do you want or need to get along with? Some people say, "I'm here to get a job done, not make friends." True, getting the job done does not require us to be friends, but it certainly helps if we can get along and work together effectively. On the other hand, we are not going to make everyone happy, and trying to do so will result in frustration. We need to be authentic and true to who we are, and doing so will result inevitably in making some people unhappy.

What can we do with the people with whom we cannot get along, no matter how we try? If they happen to be in a position where we have to deal with them, then we will have to find a way to get along with them in spite of our differences. One way to handle a difficult person is to imagine that they are your best friend and to treat them that way every day. This means you will be nice to them in spite of how they treat you. You will not retaliate or escalate if they treat you badly. You will squelch any bad thoughts if they appear to ignore or snub you. You will give them the benefit of the doubt every time. You will go out of your way to be nice to them. It is quite amazing how being nice to someone will disarm their hostility. They won't know what to do at first as your nice reaction will not be expected. It will stop them dead in their tracks and force them to reconsider their behavior. If they continue to treat you badly and you continue to be nice to them, it will become obvious to everyone around that they are the problem. You don't want to be the aggressor as this makes you look like the bad guy, and the same applies to them. If they want to continue to treat you badly, fine. This will expose them as the aggressor, and peer pressure will eventually force them to tone down their behavior. It works like a charm! They will probably never really be your best friend or even a trusted ally, but by being nice to them, you can at least neutralize them as a threat and create a peaceful environment where you and they can do your jobs. And after all, that is all you need to do—work with them enough to get your job done. You don't really need to be their friend, but you also don't want to allow a difficult relationship to derail your work or ruin your good reputation.

> The absence of conflict is not harmony, it's apathy.
> —Christopher Hoenig in *The Problem Solving Journey*

Getting another person to change their behavior is difficult to do. We want them to do something different, but for some reason, they do not want to change their behavior. Presumably, they are acting in a manner that is beneficial or natural for them.

Getting them to change because we want them to is problematic, as they may not see any reason or benefit. In this situation, there are two people, and realistically, I can impact the behavior of only one with any real certainty—and of course that is me. If I am not happy with what I am getting from another person, I need to consider first what changes I can make in my behavior in order to get a better outcome from our interaction. This may seem backward, as I want a different outcome from them. However, it will be much easier and the effort is more likely to succeed if I am the one who changes my behavior in order to improve the outcome of our interaction. Consider your expectations:

- Are your expectations realistic or even necessary?
- Can you modify your expectations to improve the success of the interaction?
- Does the other person understand your mission, vision, and values?
- Do you understand their mission, vision, and values?
- What is the basis for the conflict between you?
- Is the conflict over an expectation or a different mission, vision, or value?

Discuss these and look for the source of your conflict. Look for a common ground and consider the impact that your behavior is having on the interaction. If the difference is over the mission or vision, it can usually be cleared up by a discussion and some reasonable compromise. If your difference is over a value, then there could be a problem that will not be resolvable. Beware of people who claim that they will change their values; it is not so easy.

When you are in a difficult discussion with another person, be aware of your intentions. If the intention of your communication with them is to change them or their behavior, you may have a problem. Your communication is likely to fail, at best, or escalate the discussion into a full-blown argument, at worst. When dealing with a person that you find difficult, the last thing you want to do is make the situation between you and them worse. Telling them that you want them to change and explaining why they need to do so will be like pouring gasoline on a fire. You need to listen to them carefully while encouraging them to explain their concerns. You don't need to agree with them. In fact, you may disagree strongly. Empathize, don't agree, but make sure that they understand that you have heard them. I had a difficult time with a peer once who was strongly process oriented, while I go for results, sometimes admittedly at the expense of process. I had to go through the process with him in what for me was gory and wasteful detail but for him was necessary. We ended up at the same place that I originally proposed, but now he had process to support it, and we moved on.

Difficult people make us better. Why are they difficult? Could it be that their perspective of the world is different from ours? There is likely some learning for us in their different perspective. Their mission, vision, or values may be different from ours. Talk to them to understand their perspective. You may find that they are not so difficult after all, and the experience may help you to grow as a person and as a leader. As the leader, you will have to find a way to get along with and communicate with everyone. This doesn't mean you need to be friends with everyone, but to be an effective leader, you must be inclusive. One bad apple spoils the barrel, so you cannot allow even one person to be at odds with you and your goals. Make it a challenge to reach that difficult person and see if you can at least achieve a truce, so you can both get your jobs done.

Difficult people and difficult situations can be huge opportunities for us to show others what we are capable of. These difficulties are challenges that we can either deal with creatively and effectively or avoid. It is our choice to accept the challenge in a constructive manner and convert the situation into an opportunity where we can apply our best skills or, if necessary, improve our skills. M. F. Weiner said, "Don't waste a crisis." I paraphrase that as "Don't waste a difficult situation."

One way to diagnose how to best handle a difficult person or situation is to allow your mind to play out different scenarios in your head. Kind of like a movie, imagine yourself going into a difficult situation and imagine what could happen. Envision the worst possible outcomes that can happen in response to your action. Once you see what can go wrong, play the scenario again, but this time modify your behavior or what you say on purpose, attempting to avoid the bad outcome. Keep doing this until you have seen all the potential pitfalls and have come up with what you think is the best approach you can find to get the desired result and avoid the bad outcomes. This method can be very powerful in helping prepare you for a difficult situation. Keep it honest and avoid the temptation to be a Walter Mitty, out of touch with reality. The purpose is not to help you be a better actor but rather to help prepare you to behave in the best manner possible in a real situation that you are facing. It's called preflecting. It is like reflecting on a past situation to learn from what you did well and what you can do better next time. The only difference is that you are reflecting on a situation that hasn't happened yet. You are imagining how the situation could play out in order to learn in advance what could go right and what could go wrong so that you can handle it in the best manner possible. Preflect on a situation before it happens and reflect on it after it happens to learn as much as you can about how to handle difficult situations like this in the future.

A well-handled difficult situation can be a career-changing event. I was asked by the president of our company to present to him and the Executive Committee a quality review of our most important product. The review was positive, and my conclusion was that there was no quality concern. He listened quietly but then in his boisterous manner announced, "Oh bullshit. I don't agree." The Executive Committee members sat quietly, none venturing to come to my rescue. I could have folded or cried, but luckily for me, that morning on my drive to work, I listened to a tape on dealing with difficult situations. The advice, which I followed, was to acknowledge his statement and then explain the reasons for my conclusion. I maintained my composure and said, "John, I appreciate your opinion, but I've been working on this product for over twenty years, and from my experience, there is no quality deterioration." To my amazement, he backed down and accepted my conclusion with no further discussion! Difficult situations are opportunities dressed as problems.

Anyway

People are often unreasonable, illogical and self-centered. Forgive them anyway.

If you are kind, people may accuse you of selfish, ulterior motives. Be kind anyway.

If you are successful, you will win some false friends and some true enemies. Succeed anyway.

If you are honest and frank, people may cheat you. Be honest and frank anyway.

What you spend years building, someone could destroy overnight. Build anyway.

If you find serenity and happiness, they may be jealous. Be happy anyway.

The good you do today; people will often forget. Do good anyway.

Give the world the best you have, and it may not
be enough.
Give the world the best you've got anyway.

—originally written by Dr. Kent M. Keith as
the Paradoxical Commandments, but I like this
simpler version popularized by Gonxha Agnes
Bojaxhiu (Mother Teresa) better

Trust

Mutual trust between coworkers is the glue that holds us together, especially in times of trouble. If we trust another person, we will be much more likely to support them when times are tough and be willing to take personal risks to keep them safe. Of course, the same applies to us as well. We build trust like building a wall, one brick at a time. We can lose trust due to one event where we betray the trust that others have put in us, like a wall that falls due to an earthquake. A lot of hard work over many years can be lost in a single event. But even in something as seemingly pure as trust, there is a balance to be struck. When we trust too much or too quickly, others may take advantage of us. When we withhold trust or are overly suspicious, we may lose the opportunity to collaborate with other people.

We want people to trust us. As a leader, it is critical that people on our team trust us. We achieve that by demonstrating the behaviors that build trust—being consistent and authentic, maintaining high integrity in all that we do, being honest and forthright, admitting when we are wrong, supporting others when they ask for it, apologizing when we wrong someone, avoiding being defensive, avoiding being offensive or rude, avoiding having a hidden agenda, and so on.

We want to trust other people too. They achieve that by demonstrating to us the behaviors that build trust—being consistent and authentic, maintaining high integrity, and so on. We would be foolish and become a mark for those who would like to see us fail if we trusted everyone completely and without reason. My personal rule is not to trust anyone completely, which does not mean that the people around me are bad people or that I am paranoid in thinking that everyone is out to get me. It means that I always have a tiny antenna up looking and listening for clues about what people are saying and doing. We may think that we are transparent, but even we have a hidden agenda. The hidden agenda is what we really want to achieve, and it probably includes some personal goals that may not be in the best interest of others. We often don't tell people our hidden agenda; that's why it is hidden! I don't want you to know that the reason I am pushing for this project is that it will allow me to fly to Florida and take my kids to Disneyworld. I cannot tell you that, or it could backfire on me. Therefore, I keep my real agenda hidden and just keep pushing for the project.

> If you have integrity, nothing else matters.
> If you don't have integrity, nothing else matters.
> —Alan Simpson

Our agenda is complex and composed of our desires, wants, needs, and fears, as well as those of our spouse, kids, parents, and so on. Our agenda is like an iceberg; we only show the people around us the very tip of the iceberg, while the rest of it remains hidden below the water. The parts below the water are the most important and the most sensitive. We hide the parts of our agenda that are the most personal. Some of what we hide from others we may even hide from ourselves. Our behavior is driven by what we want to achieve, tempered by those desires and fears that are hidden below the water line. Some of those wants are more important to us than others, so we are flexible and cooperative regarding some but not all. The fact that the reasons underlying these wants are hidden makes it difficult for others to predict or understand what we are trying to achieve and can lead to misunderstanding or hard feelings. When I want to get along with you, I will try to predict and give you what you want in an encounter as long as it doesn't violate my agenda and wants. If I guess incorrectly about what you want, I will not satisfy your wants, and you will respond negatively. I then will adjust and try again based on the new information. Maybe this time I will guess better and get close enough to what you want to satisfy you, and we are now okay. Maybe I miss again, and you respond negatively again. We can keep playing this game until either you finally get what you want or one of us gives up and ends the encounter in failure. My accuracy in predicting and understanding your agenda is critical to the success of the encounter. Success first depends on your ability and willingness to express your wants (agenda) in a sufficiently clear manner that I can understand. That is not always easy to do, as you will be reluctant to express or expose the hidden parts. Second, it depends on my ability to understand your agenda and then on my willingness to give it to you. Clearly, if our mutual agendas are in conflict, we will have a problem. Generally, reasonable people can reach an acceptable agreement once they have been able to establish and communicate their agendas to each other in a clear and sufficiently complete manner. The bigger issue is usually that one or both fail or refuse to express their agenda fully, making agreement dependent on the mindreading of a hidden agenda—a tenuous game at best.

Discovering another person's hidden agenda can be challenging and fun, at least for me, by making it a bit of a detective game. Keep your eyes and ears open and watch for behavior or language that is not totally consistent with or explainable by the known facts. Consider potential unstated motivating factors. Then watch for evidence to support one or another of these potential factors. If you feel bold, ask a few clarifying questions and watch the response, both verbal and nonverbal. If you have good rapport with the person, they may tell you the truth. If you suspect that they aren't telling you the truth, that is telling too.

The fact that people have hidden agendas does not mean I cannot trust them. It just means that the situation is more complex than it appears on the surface. In fact, when dealing with people, the situation is almost always more complicated than it appears on the surface! Building mutual trust allows us to give each other some space to be ourselves, warts and all. Trust me!

> Love all, trust a few, do wrong to none.
> —William Shakespeare

Men and Women in Groups

A good way to balance a team is to include people with different strengths and perspectives. In my experience, a sure way to do that is to have a mix of men and women on the team. I think we all know by now that men and women behave and think differently. Thank God! John Gray's book, *Men Are from Mars, Women Are from Venus,*[10] is an interesting and enlightening book on the subject. A balance of men and women on a team will almost always perform better than a group composed of solely men or solely women. This seems reasonable, but the impact is much greater than you might imagine. I have seen this dynamic repeated several times in my work career and found that a monoculture of men or women was not an easy situation to manage. When a single man or woman was added to the mix, the situation improved dramatically and almost instantaneously.

A work group of only men will behave differently when a woman is added to the group. Boys will be boys! A group of men working together will bond and become very tight. They will tease, cajole, compete, fight, and support each other. Locker room behaviors may prevail with jokes and teasing. If the group stays together for an extended period of time, eventually the teasing and joking will result in bruised egos and bad feelings. Alliances and subgroups will form. Some members may be alienated and unsupported. Arguments and irreconcilable differences will result, impacting group performance. Include a woman in the group, and behaviors will change for the better. Men will behave like gentlemen when a woman is around. The joking and teasing will still be there but much damped down. Including some women in the group is a good thing for group performance.

A work group of only women will behave differently when a man is added to the group. The behavior of a group of women working together will eventually become nitpicking, critical, and destructive. Complaints and annoyances will be elevated to major conflicts. Jealousy and bickering will reduce group performance. Alliances and subgroups will form. This is especially true when the group is confined to a small office or work area where they cannot get away from each other. They have little or no personal space, conversations can be overheard, and privacy is nil. Include a man in the group, and behaviors will change for the better. Women will be more civil and less critical of each other when a man is around. Mixed-sex groups are almost always easier to manage than single-sex groups. If you are unlucky enough to inherit an unbalanced team that is composed of one sex or the other, I suggest that you find a way to mix it up.

Fun at Work

One of my personal rules about being an effective leader is to have fun and to make it fun. Balancing fun with work is effective because it creates an atmosphere where people willingly do their best work. You've probably been told at least once in your career that you are not supposed to have fun at work. I disagree most strongly with this. Fun is not only appropriate in the work place; it is essential to engaging people and getting top performance. When work is fun, people work harder and exceed expectations, taking the work to a level we may not even have envisioned. It can be a game changer. When work is not fun, it is drudgery, and people will do as little as possible or avoid the hard work completely. I like to say, "Let's work hard, be successful, and have fun—in that order!" Without hard work, there is no success. Without success, there is no fun. Without fun, there is no hard work. It is a virtuous cycle that starts with hard work.

START HERE

WORK HARD   BE SUCCESSFUL

HAVE FUN

REPEAT!

Now of course I'm not talking about inappropriate "fun" like horseplay, teasing, or telling dirty jokes. So how do we have and promote appropriate fun in the workplace? There are many ways. One way is not to take ourselves or the work so seriously. The work is serious, but we can make light of it occasionally to break the tension. Some organizations have made it part of their culture to celebrate the biggest performance goof-up of the month. Everyone recognizes that the goof-up was not the desired outcome, but as long as no one got hurt, we recovered and got the job done—let's celebrate in good fun and learn from it. It is particularly effective when the boss makes light of a tense situation. It loosens up the group. Everyone sees that no one is going to get shot or fired, and we find a way to get the job done in spite of the error or perhaps even because of it. We pick ourselves up, laugh a little, and get back to work with renewed energy and commitment.

I like to say what I am serious about in a joking manner and what I am joking about in a serious manner. A little humor makes it much easier to convey a difficult message. "Sorry, guys, but either we find a way to get this done today or nobody goes home tonight." I'm exaggerating about nobody going home tonight, but I'm not joking about the need to get the job done, and saying it as a joke gets the message across, keeps the anxiety level down, and motivates the team to get it done. And we all had a little fun doing it. And by the way, I said *nobody* goes home—and that includes me!

The goal is to communicate the tough message in a nondestructive manner that not only leaves people their dignity but builds commitment and camaraderie. As the old saying goes, "You will catch more flies with honey than with vinegar." Too many managers go through their entire career without learning that simple message. A little humor can be the sugar that makes the difficult message go down a lot easier.

Be careful with humor, as it can also be biting and hurtful. Don't overuse it. Be careful on whom you use it. Combine humor with other nonverbal cues to confirm to your people that you really are okay with them. A simple pat on the back or wink tells them that we're okay. This can be powerful stuff. Use it carefully and sincerely. See the section on authentic leadership for comments on how to be authentic and true to yourself. Using humor effectively requires that you be authentic. If you are acting, people will see through you, and it will backfire.

Conclusions on Leading Others

The best way to build a team is to develop it. If you support your people to success, they will walk through walls for you, literally. Too many leaders miss this point. They are afraid that if they teach and develop their people, it won't be long before they will start to do their job, and soon they will be out of a job. I won't say that this can never happen. It happened to me once, but I actually planned it that way. I told my boss that in three years I would work myself out of a job. He loved it. Over the next three years, I prepared my team to work without me. Then I volunteered for a more challenging job in the organization that I wanted for my own development. The fact is that the best way to learn is to teach, so we should never be afraid to teach. We actually learn more from the act of teaching others than we teach them.

Be careful when you think that you can motivate people to do anything. It is a slippery slope. Perhaps we can help them to set a higher expectation for themselves, but rarely can we get them to meet our expectations. Stating expectations is a tentative activity, and they may misunderstand due to their own screening process. The way to do this effectively is to set a goal and get them to buy into it. Goals are easier to sell than expectations.

Rewards and recognition are important tools we can use to drive and maintain performance, but they must be used carefully. Misuse can backfire on us and actually reduce performance while costing us money. We must know our people and what will excite them. It could be money. It could be praise. It could be more responsibility. It could be a bigger title or a bigger office. Don't waste your time and money on rewards that don't reward. Talk to your people and know what they want in return for better performance. Then, when they deliver, you deliver too.

Dare your people to do better. How much better? They probably know better than you do what is possible. If you treat them like professionals, they will be more likely to act like professionals. Don't doubt their abilities or intentions. Trust them, empower them, support them, let them fly, and don't allow them to fail. If you can get them to accept ownership for their work and get them to agree on goals and expectations, you can watch as they deliver the results. Reward them appropriately and dare them again, and they will find a way. Allow your people to hold each other accountable for their work. Peer pressure is one of the most powerful forces, and you as the leader don't have to get involved.

Treat everyone the same, as much as you can. Balance in how we treat people, or the perception of balance, is critical for a content workplace where jealousy and bickering are minimized. The leader has a lot of power and influence that must be used carefully and applied evenly and fairly.

Be careful with criticism, even when it is delivered with the intent of helping someone improve. Sometimes the situation requires that you take action. If you can ask a question, that is better than a direct statement. Balancing anything that even smells like criticism with a few positive statements can help. Establishing a solid rapport is certainly a requirement. Using a little humor can work well if you have that kind of rapport. Finding a way to get your people to improve their performance is one of the most rewarding things a leader can do.

Building rapport with people starts with knowing their name and using it often. Start there and then slowly get to know them.

It won't take long before you can talk to them about almost anything. There will always be at least one difficult person in the vicinity. You cannot seem to get along. Everything you do is wrong in their eyes. Turning them around will take some work. Establishing a truce where you can operate reasonably is probably a more achievable goal. But as they say, one bad apple spoils the barrel, so it is important that you find a way to detoxify them.

Trust people as much as possible until they prove themselves unworthy. Then you have a choice to make. If we cannot trust people with little things, how can we trust them with big things? Trust, like integrity, is table stakes. We need it and cannot manage very well without it. You send signals about trust in the little things you say and do. Do we trust people to take only the pens and paper that they need, or do we have a formal system to police these items? When something goes wrong, do we allow people to break the rules in order to solve the problem and support them afterward, or do we punish them regardless? Rules are rules, you know!

Leading people is a lot easier when anxiety is low, productivity is high, rules are minimal, goals are challenging, support is available, we are all successful, and we are having fun doing it. There is a great book called *Play, How It Shapes the Brain, Opens the Imagination, and Invigorates the Soul*, by Stuart Brown,[11] about the importance of play in personal development, work, and relationships. We spend too much time at work to be miserable. There are parts of every job that are at least boring if not downright odious. If the work is required to achieve our vision, finding ways to make it fun and celebrating success when it comes can make it all more worthwhile.

Chapter 4

Communication

Communication is composed of any word, action, sound, facial expression, or body language that results in another person receiving information from us. Just about everything we say and do communicates, and we need to be aware of this fact. As a leader, there is a lot we need to communicate, all the time. Of course, the mission, vision, and values need to be communicated in a clear manner and then reinforced with actions. Balance is necessary in that we don't want to talk too much but need to communicate a lot! Let's consider some of the balancing concepts.

Communicate, Communicate, Communicate!

When you have an important message, say it often in different ways, and most importantly, support it with your actions. Good communicators will usually say the important part of their message three times in different ways. Use an analogy to put the message into the context of a familiar, similar situation. Put the message into a story. Use some appropriate humor to highlight the message. Humor will often help people remember the message. Keep it simple. Force yourself to distill the important parts of your message into the shortest and simplest sentence you can come up with. The shorter the message, the more powerful it will be.

Abe Lincoln was a master at communicating with a story. He was meeting with a senator in his office to discuss an issue over the definition of some policy under consideration by the Senate. Rather than try to convince him otherwise, the president used a simple story to illustrate his point. He said, "Senator, let's suppose for a minute that we agree that a dog's tail is really a leg. Given that, how many legs does a dog have?"

The senator responded, "Well, I suppose it has five legs."

Abe replied, "Nope, four. Calling the tail a leg doesn't make it a leg." In a simple and direct manner, Abe communicated his opinion to the senator.

Effective communication is able to get past the screening process that we all do on every input. We constantly and subconsciously screen visual and auditory inputs based on our past experience. This is how magicians can fool us with their sleight of hand. Our brains complete the incomplete image we see with what we think is right. We see or hear what was never there or said. We all screen differently based on our personal, unique life experiences. That is why it is important to say the message three times in different ways—to get past the automatic mental screening process. We want other people to understand what we are communicating, and by the third time, most people will get it.

When communicating, ask for confirmation. If you have any doubt whether the person you are talking to understands what you have said, ask them to summarize the message in their own words. You may be surprised by what they heard you say. Be especially sensitive when communicating with people from different cultural backgrounds than your own. Differences in backgrounds and experience will create different screening patterns. Expect people with a different cultural background to misunderstand your message the first time. To make it even more difficult when communicating with people from other cultures, words in their language have different meanings than in yours. You may both be speaking English or whatever common language, but the words don't always have the same meaning. We think in our native language, so even if we are speaking English, they are thinking in their native language, and this will change the meaning. For example, the English word *compromise* and the Spanish word *compromiso* sound very similar, but the meaning is quite different. My Spanish-speaking amigo thinks that I am talking about a commitment when I say *compromise*, when of course I mean no such thing. Similarly, the Spanish verb *esperar* can mean expect, wait, or even hope. When I talk about an *expectation*, and they are thinking *esperar*, their word includes waiting and hoping, where my word doesn't. Observe their actions and reactions as you speak. Say the important part of your message several times in different ways and watch if they react. Ask questions to clarify and confirm their understanding. In some cultures, it is difficult to say no, especially to the boss, so if you ask someone if they can do something, the answer will always be yes. If you probe a bit and ask a specific question about the project, you may find out that they don't have the resources or the time to make it happen. However, when you asked if they could deliver on time, they said yes!

Leaders need to stand up and be heard by their followers. In the old days, a speaker would literally stand on a soapbox to allow himself to be seen and heard by the surrounding people. I suppose that method can still be effective today.

Communication, of course, is a two-way street, with the need to balance communication in both directions. If you say too much, people will be confused. If you say too little, they will be lost. If you listen too much, you will be confused. If you listen too little, you will be lost. As a leader, it will be important to your success to be able to communicate the vision and goals to your people clearly and effectively. You will also need to get feedback from your people on how the work is proceeding and how you personally are doing. People will rarely speak openly and freely to the boss. You must realize that what you hear is only part of the story. Hopefully, there are at least a few people in your organization who trust you enough to tell you the truth. Cultivate an open relationship with these people. However, don't expect even your most trusted comrade to tell you everything. If you hear any hint about what could be better, multiply it by ten to get close to what they really think. It may be good being king, but it's not easy!

Compliments

As a leader, we will need to talk to almost anyone about almost anything. Breaking the ice with a sincere, well-placed compliment can be a great way to open communication. The old saying that "flattery will get you nowhere" is absolutely false. Giving a compliment to anyone, no matter who they are, is a powerful way to build rapport and camaraderie. "Hey, John. I really like that tie!" is sure to get a smile, improve John's mood, and convince him that you are a good person who cares about him. It is a powerful way to cement a relationship based on trust and cooperation. It can work even on bosses. Bosses love compliments too. The higher the person is in the organization, the greater the risk of a compliment backfiring, so the more careful you want to be. The "nice tie" compliment will probably not endear you to the CEO; it will paint you as a suck-up. Instead, focus on their actions. For example, "I was impressed with how you allowed the team to take the lead on the Smith project. I know that wasn't easy for you," can be a great way to reinforce a positive behavior in your boss. Compliments must be honest, based on real behavior, and sincerely offered, or they will backfire and paint you as an idiot or blowhard.

Be specific when complimenting, focusing on behaviors or decisions, and avoid complimenting someone for who they are. For example, "I really like the way you handled the negotiation of the Smith project" is better than "You did well" is better than "You're good."

Subordinates especially respond positively to well-placed and specific compliments about their behavior and performance. You can sprinkle compliments liberally among your direct reports. They will rarely tire of them, as long as the compliment is about a specific event and is sincere. Avoid complimenting them more than once for a specific behavior, or they will think you are blowing smoke. Find a new event to focus on each time. Giving compliments when people perform well makes it much easier to ask them for improvement when the need to do that comes along. They will accept your request for improvement much more readily knowing that you have all along recognized them for their good performance and are aware of what is going on. It will be difficult for them to think that you don't know what you're talking about when you give them the occasional "I need your help to do this better" request.

Emails

Email is a fast, powerful, and potentially difficult means of communication. It's not a very good means of communication, as we often choose the words we use in an email carelessly, it is meant to be brief, so we don't say a lot, nobody reads it anyway, and it goes everywhere without control, to mention a few issues! In balance, we need to use email because it is fast and powerful, but we also need to recognize its limitations and not depend on email to communicate the important messages. Email can be an effective part of our balanced communication repertoire, if used carefully.

Emails are good for short, simple communications. If it is a complicated or a lengthy topic, you are probably better off picking up the phone or having a face-to-face meeting to discuss it rather than trusting an email. An email may be a good way to introduce a topic, but it is usually not a good way to gain consensus or alignment of a team or a group.

Keep in mind that once an email is sent, you cannot control where it goes. In fact, it could be forwarded almost anywhere to anyone. If it contains sensitive information, mark it confidential and state "Sensitive material—please do not forward." However, remember you have lost control and it still could end up in anyone's inbox. A good practice is to write every email considering that your boss or the president of your company will read it. If you are saying something critical about another person or group, consider that they might be reading it. This will take some of the fun out of writing emails, but it will also keep you out of trouble.

People cannot see your face in an email, so they are missing the nonverbal cues that can tell them when you are joking or being serious or inquisitive. This makes it much easier for people to misunderstand and be offended by an email communication. Emails tend to be short, which can make your communication seem terse or impatient. You may not have meant anything of the sort when you wrote it, but people on the receiving end have only the short note to go by. Be extra thoughtful and careful when you write emails. Consider how the receiving person will interpret or potentially misinterpret your email. It's good to keep emails short because people don't read long ones, but if you have something important to say (and hopefully you do, or why are you writing an email in the first place?), say it early in the email or highlight it in larger, bold, or even colored type, so that the important information stands out. Don't overdo the highlighting or you lose the impact. For example, I will put the time and date of a meeting in bold, red letters so that they cannot miss it. Avoid typing in capital letters, as people think that you are yelling at them.

Is it necessary to say, "Don't use Reply All"? I guess so, as I still see people doing it. Especially when responding to a comment, responding only to the person who sent it keeps the communication personal and low-key. Copying others on your reply puts the other person in a difficult and potentially defensive position. Unless that is your express intent, don't do it.

Negative and Positive

When communicating a message, it is possible to state the point in either a positive or a negative manner. The positive statement is always more desirable and will almost always get better results. However, there are times and situations where the negative can send a jolting message. If you want or need to shock people, then some negative messaging may be just the electric current you need. Use it sparingly and carefully.

This could be another opportunity to use humor effectively. I say something a bit shocking in a serious tone while using nonverbal clues to confirm that I am really not mad. After all, I want to shock them but not kill them. "Yikes! Look at this place. When did the bomb go off?" gets my team to look around and conclude, as I did, that the place is a mess and needs to be cleaned up. Almost always, my team, who know me, agrees and gets to work on cleaning it up. The negative message delivered in a positive way got the point across without bruising any feelings and actually made us a stronger team. When you have built a really strong team, you can say almost anything and get away with it because you have credibility and they trust you. What makes communication so much fun for me is that it is so complicated and so powerful. The stakes are high, and the rewards are too.

There are some inherently negative words that are best avoided in communications. Two of these are *should* and *need to*. We can say, "You should write a report weekly" or "You need to write a report weekly" (not any better) or "You can improve by writing a report weekly" (best). The general meaning is the same, but the last statement is stated in a positive manner and will be easier for someone to accept. Negative statements can cause anxiety, as the statement includes a judgment that implies that the other person is doing something wrong. The positive statement merely states what they can do to improve. There is no anxiety or judgment involved about what they are doing or not doing. I like to get the job done with as little effort wasted on anxiety as possible. Less anxiety means there is more energy to spend on results. Morale improves, work output increases, compliments fly, we feel good about our performance, morale improves. It is a virtuous cycle of continuous improvement. Contrast this with the other possibility; performance is poor, negative comments fly, morale declines, work output declines, morale declines. This is a death spiral. Break the death spiral of negativism with positive statements that focus on what we can do to improve.

The tone we use in communication can make a message negative or positive. Consider the difference between these examples: "Have you connected with John about the Smith project?" and "Have you and John connected on the Smith project?" The difference is quite subtle, but the former is more direct, and the latter a little more collegial. Which better fits the intent of your message? The word *you* is almost always a dangerous word to use in communication. When you say *you*, it can be blaming or judgmental and put the other person on the defensive. If you don't want them on the defensive, find a different way to say it. Instead of "When will you have the Smith report ready for my review?" consider "When will the Smith report be ready for review?" In this case, the words *you* and *my* both have a judgmental edge to them. The difference may be subtle, but the meaning will be more positive to the receiving person.

Telling a person not to do something will make them think about the negative action and may even lead them, perhaps subconsciously, to do it. Better to tell them what you want them to do and make them think about the positive action.

Verbal Self-Defense

We sometimes find ourselves in conflict with another person. They verbally attack us, and we have to decide whether and perhaps how to respond. What we say in the first few seconds after an attack will make all the difference. When we are verbally attacked, responding in a similar manner is rarely the best response, although that may be the most natural and automatic response. We will often later regret what we say in that moment of emotional tension. We feel attacked. The attack may be unfair or unprovoked. Maybe we weren't even the person who caused the other person's anger. They are clearly wrong, and we are clearly right! Our egos are bruised, and we want justice—now.

Whatever the cause, the fact is that we were attacked verbally and we may feel the need to do something. Of course, we can choose not to respond, and that is in itself a viable response. The old saw to count to ten usually doesn't work, as we are too upset—and besides, if we wait too long, the moment to respond is lost. As in any fight-or-flight moment, our bodies react by pumping out adrenaline, increasing our blood pressure and heart rate. Our bodies' defense mechanisms are gearing up to either fight or run away as fast as we can. The rush of adrenaline can make it very difficult to respond rationally. The attacking person may even leave the scene, and we lose our chance to say anything. If we respond, it would be best if we were able to respond in a positive and constructive manner. To do that, we need to practice verbal self-defense.

The rules of verbal self-defense are similar to those for physical self-defense. We want to use the other person's power against them. We want to deflect their power away from us to protect ourselves from injury and further attack. Ideally, we want to stop the attack without harming ourselves or the attacker. How do we do that? Start simply by acknowledging the attack. Don't agree with the attack; just acknowledge it.

- "Can you explain your thinking please?"
- "I see you have a strong opinion on this topic."
- "I hear what you are saying."

Acknowledging the attack gives you time to assess the situation and get your emotions under control. It also gives your verbal attacker a little time to assess their situation, get their emotions under control, and possibly stop or retract the attack. At least they see that you have deflected their attack, are not hurt by it, and are strong enough to maintain your composure and respond rationally. This alone will often unnerve even the strongest verbal attacker. They are not expecting you to deflect their attack and respond rationally. They will begin to think that attacking you verbally wasn't such a good idea—and that is exactly your goal.

Once you have acknowledged the attack, your next step is to align yourself with them and not against them.

- "I can see why you might be upset."
- "I understand this is important to you."
- "I can see your point."

You align with them, not against them. You don't have to and probably don't want to agree with them. They will not expect you to acknowledge and align with them, so this will further confuse them, defuse the energy of their attack, and reduce their interest in further attacking you.

Begin to move them away from the situation and in the direction you want them to go.

- "Can I explain to you what I did here?"
- "Would it be okay if I showed you what I was doing?"
- "Can we talk about this?"
- "I've done a lot of work in this area and would like to share some of what I found."

Start to move them away from the attack mode and into alignment with you. The two of you may still disagree, but now at least you can begin to talk about it rationally and work toward understanding each other's position and actions in an unemotional manner. During this discussion, you slowly move them to align with you and to acknowledge what you were doing. This can be a very positive and powerful technique. It can work on anyone at any level of the organization. If they don't want to listen to anything you have to say, then your options are limited. You don't want to reescalate the discussion back into conflict, so start the process over by acknowledging their reluctance to listen and leave it at that. It's quite possible that they will realize that they are the problem and open up after several iterations. What do you have to lose?

They will learn from this event that you are not a person to attack verbally. You will both walk away with a better understanding of each other. Don't be surprised if you become friends after an interchange like this! It is a powerful way to earn another person's respect. Best of all, it works on anyone at any level in the organization no matter how powerful they are. Use it with a subordinate, and they will respect you for not blasting them back as your higher position could allow you to do. Use it with a peer, and they will learn that you are someone to be reckoned with. Use it with a superior in the organization, and they will respect you for your self-control and will never use authority to blast you again. It actually works best on bullies and bosses, as they will treat you more carefully in the future after seeing you deflect and survive their strongest verbal attack!

Talking and Listening

Good communication requires that we talk and listen in the proper balance. Unfortunately, listening is often not a skill that leaders actively develop in themselves. And too often, subordinates do not tell the boss what they are really thinking or feeling, so there may not be a lot to listen to. Communication to the boss is often highly filtered or nonexistent, making it easy for the boss to become out of touch with the reality that his or her subordinates are facing. The boss needs to listen hard and search for little clues in people's speech and behavior. Listen to what people say, pay attention to what they do not say, and observe their body language. If their body language is inconsistent with what they are saying, they are likely leaving something unsaid. Keep in mind that what you hear or see is only a fraction of what is really on their mind. It takes a little mind reading to listen hard, watch carefully, consider how you would feel in their situation, and then confirm. Even your most trusted associate, who professes to tell you like it is, is probably filtering the message. The flip side of that coin is that everyone has an agenda, and they cannot communicate without their personal agenda coloring the content at least a little. So not only are you getting only part of the story, the part you get is probably tilted a bit toward the teller's agenda. Listen, observe, consider the source and the potential agenda, and then confirm. Good listening skills are critical, and you almost cannot listen too much. Especially keep in mind that you cannot listen when you are talking.

We need to talk too, of course. In fact, the best way to get others to talk to us is for us to talk to them. But talking too much can be dangerous and often gets us into trouble. Perhaps we say something that we really didn't mean. Or the other person misinterprets what we say in a negative manner that we didn't intend. The trick to talking in a balanced way is to make your point and then shut up. Don't oversell. Don't defend. Don't dominate the conversation. After about twenty seconds, the other person isn't listening to you anymore anyway. The higher the position of the person you are speaking to, the less you want to talk and the more you want to listen. You may want to take advantage when you have a rare chance to talk one on one to a person who is above you in the organization, but above all, you need to listen. The more you talk, the less they will listen and the more convinced they will be that you have nothing important to say.

Many of us are uncomfortable with silence in a conversation, so we start talking again when the other person doesn't respond in a few seconds. Don't. Make your point clearly and concisely, then wait. Let the awkward silence hang there if necessary. They will respond, eventually. Give them time and let them respond.

> Most of the time we don't talk to understand
> each other, we just take turns talking.
> —Buddha

There is an important difference between communication and talking. As we have discussed, communication can almost not be overdone. In fact, communicating the key messages needs to be done often and well. Talking is another issue! We don't want to appear terse or impatient, and we don't want to be glib or dominate the conversation, requiring a balance in how much we talk and how much we listen. This is another reason why having a really short vision statement is so powerful; it allows us to say a lot with just a few words.

Another advantage of talking less is that the fewer words you use in a communication, the less chance there is of saying a wrong word or using a word that the other person may misinterpret. Keep your communications short, sweet, and to the point. Avoid using big or complicated words unless there is no simpler choice. Keep in mind that their misinterpretation of your communication can be innocent or intentional, depending on their agenda. The more words you use, the more likely it is that you will use a word they don't like and allow them the opportunity to disagree or divert the discussion in a different direction from where you intended, if that is their intent. Verbal diarrhea is not a good communication choice!

It is a sign of wisdom to be thoughtful and concise in what you say. This is a communication skill worth developing. Taking some time before you speak has several advantages: it will give you time to think, perhaps enabling you to say what you really want to say, and it will give your words more weight when you do say them. Naturally, this can be overdone too. You don't want to appear ponderous and aloof with long, pregnant pauses all the time. And, in some cultures, talking is how we build rapport and trust. Short, concise statements can appear cold or detached to people in those cultures. But when the gravity of the situation supports it, take your time before speaking. Then speak slowly and concisely. This will also give you more time to think and watch the reaction of your audience. Remember that your communication is only as good as the response it gets. Take responsibility for what people hear and understand you say.

There is an important distinction between making a point and being defensive. You don't want to be defensive in a discussion. It is a position of weakness that gives the other person all the advantages. If someone challenges you, rather than defending, sidestep the attack by saying something like "Your point is well taken. I have done work on that issue and can update you if you would like." If you don't have the facts, say so. "I understand your question but am not sure about the details. Please allow me to gather the facts and get back to you by tomorrow." This is much better than going into a long explanation based on partial facts and speculation. Even if you do know the answer and have all the facts at your fingertips, it is often better to respond in a short, positive manner now and offer to get back to them later with the full story. They will often forget about it. You didn't go for the bait, didn't get hooked by their barb, and swam away—taking all the fun out of it for them and saving yourself from getting into a mess.

A good rule for talking—if you find yourself needing to take a deep breath while talking, you are probably talking too much! Any communication of more than a few sentences is lost on the receiver and only convinces them that you are either a windbag or have something to hide. I conducted an interview once by phone.

I was in the car with my boss and his boss as we were driving to a meeting. I timed it perfectly, as we sat in New York City traffic for almost an hour while I was on the phone interview. I started to ask the person my usual list of questions but only got through a few of them, as his answers were so long and rambling. Finally, I needed to know if this guy could actually answer a question concisely if his life depended on it. I asked him very deliberately. "John, I'm looking for a short answer please, twenty-five words or less. No more than twenty-five words please." He talked for five minutes. I put him on mute, and we all laughed. The interview was over.

> If you find yourself in a hole, stop digging!
> —Will Rogers

Talking less is almost always better than talking more.

Delivering Bad News

There are times when we must give someone bad news, hopefully work related and not personal. How we communicate the bad news is critical to what the other person hears, how they receive it, what they do about it, how well they recover from it, and ultimately what they think about us.

When reporting bad news to our boss or another superior, state the facts as succinctly as you can and identify the options to solve the problem. Don't hit them with just the bad news. And don't wait so long that there is risk they will find out about it from someone else. Hopefully you already have started to work on the solution. Keep to the point and do not wander into other topics. You will probably not impress them by talking about all the good work you have done, even though it is true. If the results don't measure up to expectations, all the good work and good intentions in the world don't count. Focus on the issue and the solution. Make it clear that you are fully aware of the issue, know what to do about it, and have a plan to get it done. If there are costs, present them honestly. Don't lowball the cost. It's better to present a worst-case estimate with some real reasons to be optimistic about doing better. Don't leave out issues; get it all on the table at once. Coming back later to tell them more bad news will make you look like an idiot and destroy what credibility you still have. Then go out and execute your plan—and make sure it delivers.

We had a project to produce a croissant, and my team was charged with developing the specifications for the makeup part of the production line. One critical part of the process was sizing the dough cutter. The cutter is a cylindrical unit with knives for cutting the dough sheet as it rolls underneath. It is made from a single piece of stainless steel and cost, at the time, $40,000. We did lots of experiments to make sure we got the dimensions right. And we (I) screwed it up royally. I forgot that the dough sheet would be under tension when it was cut, and therefore it would shrink in size. When we started up the line, it quickly became obvious that the cutter was sized too small. I had to go to my boss and deliver the bad news and the good news that we knew why we screwed up and had a solution. Unfortunately, the solution meant a new cutter at a cost of $40,000. My boss didn't say a word beyond "Order it." Phew!

Sometimes we need to give bad news to a subordinate. In this situation, it is best to give it to them straight. Don't beat around the bush or look for diversionary topics. Balance the negative with a good dose of the positive. Focus on their behavior and the results, not on them as a person. Bad results do not make them bad people. Bad results are not acceptable. Stick to the communicated expectations and the facts regarding performance. If you had miscommunicated or in any way were responsible for the poor results, admit your involvement. Be honest and authentic with them. Then talk about the consequences. A difficult lesson for many people is that our actions and performance have consequences. Our good looks and genial personality are great assets but don't mitigate poor results in business. We need to deliver the results or expect to suffer the consequences. Consequences don't always mean disciplinary action or being fired. Poor results can be educational and could be an investment in a person if they are capable of learning from the experience. When Thomas Watson was president of IBM, he told a senior manager who had lost millions of dollars on a failed venture that he was not going to fire him, as he had expected, but rather that this had been an expensive investment in his development as a senior leader.

Timing can be important to the success of a communication, regardless of the audience. Now may not be the right time to raise an issue. Tomorrow may not be so great either. The challenge is to recognize the right time, when the people who are going to be impacted by our efforts will be ready to listen or accept what we are proposing. Maybe we can prepare them in advance by presenting parts of the problem for them to consider. Perhaps we can ask for their help so that they can consider the issue and potential solutions. This can also prepare them mentally. Perhaps we can float a draft proposal for them to consider. A fully developed proposal sent cold to someone can put them on the defensive if they are impacted by the proposal. Once they go defensive, it will be difficult getting them to come around to support our proposal. Asking them for their help in solving a problem early on is a great way to get them involved in the issue and getting our proposal to be their proposal as well.

Abraham Lincoln knew the value of timing. He wrote the Emancipation Proclamation and carried it in his pocket for a full year before he felt the time was ready to share it with his cabinet. In that year, he prepared his cabinet for the radical proposal he was going to make in the proclamation. There were many controversial and difficult issues to be dealt with before the proclamation could be a success. He spent that year preparing his cabinet, Congress, and the public, and when the time was right and they were ready, he acted and was successful. Chances are if he had presented it sooner, he would have met severe criticism and failed instead of succeeding.

Reframing

Reframing is listening to a message, typically one that we don't particularly want to hear, and changing it into a message that we can deal with effectively. When we get a message that we don't like, we can reject it, accept it grudgingly, or reframe it into a message that makes sense to us. Reframing doesn't deny the message but puts it into a form that has meaning to us, so we can process it. Does that sound easy? It's not easy, but it's a technique that can help us to maintain our balance and even excel in a difficult situation.

It is amazing how a negatively stated, emotionally charged request can put us on the wrong track. We will be frustrated and feel that the boss is an idiot who doesn't understand us. We have worked hard to establish the optimal balance in leading our team, and the boss doesn't get it. If we fail to respond appropriately, the boss will be frustrated with our apparent lack of response to their request and think that we are inept. All this wasted energy and lack of performance can be due to the lack of a positively framed request.

Reframing is often beneficial to help us to deal effectively with a message from our boss. None of us are perfect communicators, and communications between a boss and subordinate are especially difficult. Communications may be strained by past experiences, hidden agendas, or even imagined issues on both sides. We do not always communicate in a clear and positive manner, so what we communicate may not be easy to understand by the other person. We say what we think we mean, but our manner of speaking and body language communicate the negative or positive emotions we are feeling, which could be different from what we are saying. People also hear what they want to hear based on their personal mental screening, meaning that they may not hear exactly what we said. In addition, emotions will impact interpretation of what people hear and how they feel about it. Does this mean that good communication between a boss and a subordinate is impossible? Almost! If we expect perfect and positive communication from our bosses, we will be sorely disappointed.

One way to improve this difficult situation is for us to learn how to reframe what our boss says in words and emotions that are meaningful to us. We must dig into the communication to understand what motivated it in order to understand what the boss is really saying. If this sounds like mind reading, in a way it is, but if we know the boss, their values, and something about the situation, we can use these to provide a context to more accurately interpret and understand what we are hearing, seeing, and feeling in the communication from them. It is critical not to act only on what we hear the boss saying—we might have misunderstood or misinterpreted. Remember we hear what we *want* to hear. If the communication is going to be successful, we must hear what they meant to say and then act on it. This requires that we be aware of our own screening and our own agenda, as these will influence our interpretation. The boss is probably not a perfect communicator. And we are not a perfect listener. Communication is tough work, both sending and receiving! It is also critical and necessary work. Working to get it right on both the sending and receiving end is worth the extra effort. Let's look at some real examples to help make this easier to understand.

When the boss asks you to do something and you feel yourself resisting the request for any reason, you need to ponder—what is the reason for your resistance? Maybe you don't want to do what they are asking you to do, or perhaps you think there is a better way to get the job done. The important thing for now is to be aware that you feel resistance; that is the clue. Maybe you don't understand why they are asking you to do something that you feel is wrong or unnecessary. Maybe they really are crazy or out of touch with reality—your reality. Don't react negatively or put up a fight. Ask clarifying questions if you are able to. If you cannot ask questions in a controlled manner or are done with that, get away so you can think.

We need to figure out what the boss is really asking for. What is the situation? What is the result with which they are not satisfied? What needs to be done to correct the situation? Once you have some answers, restate in a positive manner what the boss is really asking for. Now work on fixing that situation. If you can restate their request (the one that you did not like) in a positive fashion that you can understand and deal with in a constructive manner, then you have successfully reframed their request.

The boss says, "You know, Len, I think we need to do something different on safety. Can you have a plan on how you will restructure the teams to me by next week?" I'm thinking, *He doesn't have a clue about all the hard work I've done in this area for the past year. Not only that, but I think the program and teams we have in place now are the best way to handle the job—that's why I designed them the way they are. To change it now would risk the entire program. How do I tell him that and convince him that no changes are needed now?*

Sounds like a good opportunity for reframing. First, what is motivating the boss to say what they said? Is there a performance issue? Identify the desired result and reframe the question around it. The program is good, but we have not been able to achieve the incident rate we targeted. Okay, so perhaps the issue is getting the incident rate down. What can we do to bring down the safety incident rate faster? Now you have positively stated the issue, without implying that you haven't done your job, while focusing on what you can do to improve. You have reframed the issue in a positive, de-emotionalized, and depersonalized manner, and now you can figure out what you can do and how to do it. You are happy, and the boss will be happy with your positive attitude and performance improvement. That is successful reframing.

If all else fails, ask yourself, "What is the right thing to do for the business?" (Thanks, Gary Prince!). Forget your ego, invested effort, existing systems, plans, and momentum for a moment. What is the right thing to do for the business? Identify the desired end result and the steps needed to get there. Now go back to the boss and show them what you are going to do to resolve the issue and explain how it is right for the business. When you do this, don't spend more than a minute telling them about all the good things you have done; chances are they already know. What they want to hear, in a nondefensive and positive manner, is what you are going to do next and when.

Good reframing is self-motivating and puts you back in charge. Sometimes we are so close to the answer, but emotion and misunderstanding create a fog that prevents us from seeing what is sitting right there in front of us. Don't let anyone take your mojo away!

> The blindest man is the one who does not want to see.
> —Mexican saying

As the boss, you can save your direct reports from the wasted effort of reframing by being acutely aware of the potential impact that your requests have on them. What vested interests do your direct reports have in the issue? How much investment of time and effort do they have in the particular position or program that you are now asking them to change? At a minimum, you can acknowledge their interest and the work they have done. "John, I recognize that you have spent the last year optimizing the structure of your department and have shown real improvement. I'm asking you to evaluate it once again in the light of our new performance expectations. Do we still have the right structure in place to get it done?" Acknowledge past efforts and progress and then put out the challenge to look at it again. This keeps everyone whole and focuses the work on the future, not the past. No negative emotion or judgment about personal performance to be overcome. Just a clear and positively stated challenge that will require no reframing.

The Story of the Three Umpires
The youngest umpire says, "Some is strikes and some is balls, and I calls 'em like they is."
The more experienced umpire says, "Some is strikes and some is balls, and I calls 'em like I sees 'em."
The veteran umpire says, "Some is strikes and some is balls, but they ain't nothing until I calls 'em."
—Bill Klem

Conclusions on Communication

Communication is about sending an important message, so it is difficult to overcommunicate. Communication is not only about talking or emailing. It's about sending a message. Talking is one way to send the message, but there are many others that are likely more important and more effective, such as your actions, your support of the team, not allowing members to fail, your authenticity, your integrity, your commitment, and so on. Consider the quality of your communication based on the response it receives. If the target audience gets the message, then you have done a good job. If they are missing the point or misunderstanding the message, the problem is not theirs, it is yours. Change your communication. If it's not working, keep changing it until it works.

Give compliments to people when they deserve them. They will love it. Be careful with emails and go out of your way to be sensitive and clear in your emails. Remember that anyone could read your email, because once you hit the send button, you have lost control of it. A positive communication will almost always be more effective and better received than a negative one. Find a way to state your concerns in a positive, constructive manner. Humor can help soften the blow, but be careful or people could think that you are laughing at them, and this will kill any attempt at constructive communication. When you are attacked verbally, practice verbal self-defense where you deflect the attack and then move your opponent slowly into alignment with you. You will turn a potential enemy into a friend and ally. Above all, talk to people! Learn, remember, and use their names when you address them. They will be impressed that you took the time, especially the "little" people who are often forgotten. Speak your mind when the opportunity arises and you are sure of your facts.

One of the most important points about being a good communicator is to be a good listener. If you listen to people— really listen—and appreciate their feedback and ideas, you will find that they also pay more attention to yours. Listening is a two-way street. Failing to listen tells others that you already know everything and that they are wasting their time talking to you. Remember that talking to the boss or telling the boss anything, especially of a critical nature, is risky, and most people will not take the risk unless there is a good reason, such as they hope that you might actually listen and act on it.

Yes, you do need to sell your ideas. It is not a dirty job or beneath you to do so. When reporting bad news, do so in a direct, concise manner. If you want to survive to fight another day, identify the failure, accept responsibility, identify the corrective actions, and deliver. Reframe negative communications from others, attempting to understand the real underlying cause, and put it into a positive frame that you and your team can better accept and manage. Then buy them a copy of this book!

Timing is an important part of communication. Preparing your audience so that they are mentally prepared for what you have to say is a good idea, especially if it requires them to change their behaviors. People naturally resist change, so you have to prepare them so that they are not shocked. Then sell them on what you need them to do.

Effective communication is difficult, complicated, challenging, and critical to success, especially for leaders. We all think that we are better communicators than we actually are. A strong dose of humility and a little healthy paranoia can help you to more effectively evaluate your communication capabilities and help you figure out how to improve.

Chapter 5

Balance in Challenge

As leaders, we need to constantly challenge ourselves and our teams to perform ever better—but in balance. Challenge for the sake of challenge can be a waste of time, whereas, if we get the balance right, it can be a powerful way to keep ourselves and our organizations fresh and current. We need to consider our mission, vision, and values, balanced against our skills and resources, all seasoned with a strong dose of reality. Some challenges we get to create, while others may come to us without our approval. Lastly, how we communicate the challenge to our team can make a significant difference.

Challenge

Challenges come in many forms. Consider for a moment the activities that people like to engage in for fun or recreation. Golf, gambling, hiking, team sports, hunting, camping, boating, exercise, gardening, painting, photography, skiing, tennis, bowling, crossword puzzles, and chess are a few that come to mind. The common element that makes all of these activities fun is that they all involve some degree of challenge. People like a challenge, and they like to compete. Challenge motivates performance and improvement. It can be applied effectively to work and can be a powerful reward and incentive in itself. Most of us come to work for a practical reason—we need a paycheck. The lucky ones among us are the ones who get a paycheck for doing what we enjoy doing. People who are able to find or create challenge in their work and do what is necessary to be successful experience the ultimate reward—success. Nothing feels better than success against a respectable challenge to make work enjoyable. People love to work for leaders who create reasonable challenges and then help them to be successful. Teams led by challenge achieve great results.

The concept of balance plays heavily into this analysis. Too much challenge makes the work drudgery, which leads to failure, the ultimate de-motivator. Too little challenge causes the work to be boring, so people lose interest, again leading to failure and demotivation. The right amount of challenge leads to a positive result that rewards the doer and motivates future performance. Support success with adequate preparation and appropriate resources. The balance of challenge, support, and coaching that we choose will depend greatly on the situation, the person being challenged, and on you the challenger.

As the leader, you want to provide the appropriate level of challenge, support, and coaching for your people. For example, people might enjoy playing basketball in the backyard or at a local gym with friends or family. How much fun would it be to take our weekend hoop shooter and challenge them by putting them into a professional basketball game? It might be a great honor and a great experience for about thirty seconds until our unprepared and underskilled person gets trampled by the professional players. It would not be fun at all, and they could get seriously hurt.

The challenge must be appropriate to the skill level and ability of the person being challenged. Otherwise, it will not be fun, rewarding, or motivational. This means that we must assure that the person has had adequate preparation in the form of training and experience (also called practice). It means having the proper tools as well. Our job as the leader is to support our people by making sure that they have the resources they need to be successful. Create a reasonable level of challenge, provide the necessary resources, support people to success, increase the challenge, and repeat until the desired level of performance is achieved. This is the way to turn around a weak performer, turn a good performer into a star, or keep a star a star.

Our work and careers are important to most of us. When you introduce yourself, do you say your name and what you do for a living? If so, you are normal. We define ourselves by what we do, especially if we are good at and proud of what we do. Success in our work and ability to perform under reasonable levels of challenge actually defines who we are as people and as members of society. Success in our work is important to us as people and as leaders. As a leader, it is important that you know how your people define themselves and what kinds of challenges motivate them.

- What activities or abilities are they most proud of?
- What achievements are they most proud of?
- How can you create a healthy and meaningful challenge for your people?

The other side of the challenge coin is routine. We all need a certain amount of routine in our lives, or we will drive ourselves crazy. Challenging yourself to brush your teeth in a different or better manner every morning might be fun, or it might create anxiety you just don't need early in your day. Having a stable, comfortable routine for many of the activities that we do every day gives us a framework to build on. One problem people face when they retire is that their old routine of many years is no longer appropriate, and they flounder and fall into bad habits. They need to establish a new routine. Routines are important, and so is challenge—both in proper balance.

Challenge in the extreme is demand. Many leaders think that they must be demanding of their direct reports. They think, *If I don't demand good work, I won't get it. People are naturally lazy and will do as little work as they can get away with, if I let them.* The boss must demand and constantly oversee the work. If this is the kind of work environment you want for yourself and your people, go ahead and be demanding. You will get what you demand, most of the time. You will not get much more than you demand, and you will stifle self-initiative and creativity. There is a big difference between demanding and challenging. When I am demanding, the responsibility to define the work stays with me. When I am challenging, I give the responsibility for the work to the other person. I have to allow them some flexibility in defining the work, but by doing so, I take a burden off myself, freeing me up to do other things. If it is a proper challenge and they have the resources, skills, and time to get the job done, and they accept the challenge, the job will get done, and everyone wins. Involve your people in defining the challenge to encourage ownership and to build mutual trust.

A good way to tell if you are challenging yourself and your people appropriately is to ask a few questions:

- Are you and your people more capable at important and relevant skills today than a year ago?
- Are you and your people bored or energized by your work tasks?
- Do you and your people want to come to work each day or have Monday depression?

- How is the stress level in your organization?
- Does work get done in an efficient manner, or is there a lot of unnecessary anxiety?
- When a challenge arises, how natural is it for you to ask your team to step up their game?
- Do they deliver? How natural is it for the team to pull together to rise to the challenge?
- Do you lead or manage the challenge?

Ask people for their help in achieving a goal. You cannot do everything yourself, and you don't want to try. Build your team by asking the team members to help. Walk into the midst of the group and say, "Guys, I need your help. I just found out that we won a bid on a special rush project. I need everyone to put your current work on hold for a few days and pitch in to get this done. I appreciate that this will cause some inconvenience for all of us, but it is a new and important customer, with big potential for the future, so we need to do this right. Will you please do this?" People will rally together and jump at the chance to help the boss and make the company look good. Asking them as a group guarantees that they will hold each other accountable to get it done. Now when they come through, make a point to compliment them and thank them for their extra effort. This is how you challenge, build the team, and lead the team to a good result. Notice that you did not manage the team. You asked for their help. They did the work. They managed the result. All you did was provide the leadership. This is a critical and important point to see. You did not manage. You led. That freed you up to do your job. It freed up the team to do their job and grow in the process. The recognition at the end of the positive result puts a bow on the package and builds team rapport for the next challenge that is lurking around the corner. Lead the challenge—do not manage the challenge!

Change

Related to challenge is change. Don't fear change. Embrace and lead change. Use change as a competitive advantage both in your personal life and in business. Walt Disney said, "Don't predict the future, invent it." The opposite of change is stagnation. We don't want to stagnate. Too many people stay in the same job for too long and get bored, tired, or in a rut from doing the same thing the same way over and over. There are some people who can do the same job for many years and yet are not bored with it. How do they do that? They do it by bringing a perspective of change to their work. It may look like they are doing the same job today that they did five years ago or longer, but they have made improvements and adjustments in what they do to make it different and interesting. They challenge themselves every day to meet or exceed their past performances, and in this way, they keep the work fresh and new. One way to do this is to make a game of your work, keep score, and find ways to improve your score every day.

We must be the change in the world that we want.
—Mahatma Gandhi

Are you changing or improving fast enough to keep ahead of your competition? If not, then eventually you will fall behind them. The world is changing rapidly. There is evidence that, in many aspects, the rate of change is increasing. I have often thought that we are living in unique times and that the current rapid rate of change is not sustainable, so therefore, at some point change will slow down and some stability will be achieved. I realize now that I was wrong in this thinking. Change will not slow down because too many people and organizations now drive change as a strategic weapon. If we can change or improve faster than our competitor, then we will surpass and beat them. The insidious nature of change is that it is continuous and incremental. The result over time is substantial and game-changing. The last thing you want to do is wake up one day to realize that your competition is far ahead of you. Catching up is not easy or fun. If you are not improving or changing as fast as or faster than your competition, then you will eventually find yourself in this position. What new skills or capabilities do you need to develop to keep up or keep ahead? Technology is changing rapidly. It is a total copout to say, "I'm too old to learn how to use this new technology." You can of course, as a senior manager, delegate such work to the young kids on your team. This might be perfectly acceptable and practical. However, you need to at least be aware of and understand the basics of the new technology in order to drive it in your team or organization. Change is never comfortable. But then neither is losing. Keep a sharp eye on technology and on your competition and keep up, or even better, drive the change initiatives to keep yourself, your team, and your organization in the lead. Let your competition play catch up to you. Set the agenda. Set the pace. Create the need. The only balance in managing change is making sure that you are not behind. The best place for your competition is in your rearview mirror!

It is not the strongest of species that survives, nor the most intelligent, but the ones that are most responsive to change.
—Charles Darwin

Sometimes you need to make a radical change in structure, perhaps resulting in a reduction in the workforce. This is one of the most difficult changes to lead a team through successfully. It can be critical to the success or survival of your team or organization to lead them successfully through a reduction in force. It can be gut-wrenching to lay off people you have worked with for years and love. Read the now classic book on the subject, *Reengineering the Corporation* by Michael Hammer and James Champy,[12] for great insight into the process and how to get through it. There are a few key concepts to consider. First, involve your people in the process to decide where and how to cut. You will be amazed at the response if this is an open and transparent process. Don't expect people to volunteer to be cut, but if you have been honest with them, they will cooperate and make the painful process more effective and more humane for all. When the job cuts are decided, do it quickly and at one time. Don't draw it out or keep people in suspense. Uncertainty is highly destructive. People deserve to know what their fate is, so that they can make decisions and get on with their lives. Be clear about any severance or services to which they are entitled.

Once the cuts are made and the people are gone, attend to the survivors. It is natural for them to mourn the loss of their friends, coworkers, and even the budget cut that may accompany the reduction in force. They will think, *We had a tough time getting the job done before when we had a larger staff and budget. How are we ever going to get the job done now? It is impossible.* It is the job of the leader to get them past this negative thinking. Identify the issues, prioritize, and then help the team to be successful in one aspect of the job at a time until they get past it. Help them by breaking up the work and assigning ownership. Getting people to own the work allows them to focus their efforts to get one part of the work done successfully, and allows them to get better at it. Getting better allows them to find ways to get the work done well with less time, effort, and money. Focusing on getting the work done better and on being successful will help them get past the mourning stage. Reducing the size of the staff will in many ways make the work easier, as there are now fewer people to involve and coordinate with when doing the job. This will come as a pleasant surprise to all involved. It is now clearer to them that if the job is going to get done, they are going to have to do it—there is no one else! Make it a challenge, one area at a time. Ask people to take ownership and learn how to get the job done well in spite of the reductions. You will soon hear comments from them like "I can't believe how much easier it is to get the job done," "I can do this," and "You were right; we can do this." Make sure everyone knows why the cuts were made—to reduce spending so that the organization can compete and survive. In that context, they can understand why and can get back to work and find ways to get the job done with fewer people and less money. It will not happen just because they understand why. You as the leader must help them succeed. You must help them get past the negative thinking and to realize "We can do this." It is a positive team- and confidence-building experience when they get there.

Changes come in different sizes, ranging from small, incremental change to extreme, crisis changes. A crisis is a situation of extreme change, requiring special leadership skills to turn it into an opportunity and success. It is often in crisis that inspirational leaders come forward to lead the group to a new solution. This is a true and powerful statement; however, it makes me ask the question, How did the group get into the crisis situation in the first place? The answer is often a lack of leadership. A lack of leadership put us on the path to crisis, creating the opportunity for an inspirational leader to resolve it. What if we got the balance of leadership right in the first place and were able to avoid the crisis situation?

To improve is to change; to be perfect is to change often.
—Winston Churchill

Small, incremental changes appear to be the most manageable, while radical, crisis change is uncomfortable and difficult. Groups prefer the status quo, so, paradoxically, we often avoid making the necessary, small, incremental changes until they build up and require radical change. The problem with slow, incremental change is that we often don't see the negative side effects creeping up. If we are running a business—and all groups must remember that they are essentially a business and therefore must operate with fiscal responsibility—then slow, incremental increases in the cost of doing business will eventually result in the business no longer being a viable operation. Whether the group is the US Postal Service, a local fire department, a school, a library, a restaurant, a small department, or IBM, increasing costs due to the rising cost of labor, taxes, medical benefits, commodities, and so on must be dealt with, or the eventual result will be that the group is no longer a viable operation. Usually the costs creep up slowly over a period of years until a crisis situation is created and action becomes necessary. Then leadership comes forward to communicate the situation to the group and enlist their help in making the necessary cuts or redesign of the group to bring costs back into line. The change at this point is radical and painful. Leadership must convince the group members of the severity of the situation to enlist their help in implementing the redesign. Failure to make effective change at the crisis point could be disastrous. If effective changes are made, things go back to a new normal again for another period of time until the group creeps up on the next crisis. Real, good leadership would help the group make smaller, timelier adjustments in productivity or structure to offset the rising costs as they occur, in order to prevent a crisis situation from occurring. This kind of leadership is more difficult, as it is not easy to convince the group that change is needed. The increase in cost appears to be small enough to be absorbed and not require painful change at this time. There is no obvious crisis today. Waiting will only make matters worse, allowing multiple, incremental increases in cost to build up until the point of crisis is reached. Then leading the group to change is paradoxically easier, in the sense that it is easier to convince the group that change is needed when we are facing a real crisis. Does that seem backward to you?

Here is an example of how small, incremental changes, in the form of rising cost, can result in a crisis. Let's imagine a small company that has revenue of $100 million annually, total costs of $85 million, and a makes a profit of $15 million EBIT—not a bad little business. Please forgive if I take a little liberty with the math to make this example simple, if not rigorously correct. If next year, the cost of doing business increases from $85 million to $90 million, and our sales do not change—we make the same amount of product and generate the same revenue—then profit in year two will drop to $10 million—still not a bad business performance. If in year three, another similar increase in costs occurs, profits will drop again by $5 million to $5 million. Well, perhaps at this point, leadership at the company realizes that we have a problem approaching. Another year of similar cost increases will result in the company profit dropping to zero. What has happened here? Our nice little company in only four years of modest 5 percent cost increases has gone from a healthy profit of $15 million per year to bankruptcy. Now we have a crisis that must be dealt with urgently and severely. How could we have prevented this? We could have increased the cost of our product by the same 5 percent each year and maintained our profit. That would require that we pass along the cost increases to our customers. They will experience the same issue we did as their costs increase and at some point will no longer be able to afford our product. Passing along the cost to our customers is often not possible and probably not wise. Another option would be to find ways to reduce the cost of our operation each year by 5 percent to balance the cost increases and maintain profit. This is a much better approach, as it maintains the price to our customers, increasing the likelihood that we will be able to sustain or even increase sales. This takes real leadership, especially early in the game when there is no obvious crisis.

I keep an eye out for creeping, incremental change and keep my people as informed as possible about issues or changes that I see coming. I start months in advance sometimes. As soon as I get a hint that there is a change in direction coming, I tell them about it so they can prepare themselves mentally. This way, they are aligned with me and the situation. When the time comes for us to do something that we may not want to do, they are prepared and not surprised. The worst that can happen is that my warning was a false alarm; my concerns don't materialize, and we don't need to make any big changes—not so bad. Informing them ahead of time makes sure that the issue doesn't come as a surprise to them. I have given them time to absorb the potentially bad news, and they have had time to formulate options. I find if I keep them informed, when the time to act arrives, they are either with me or ahead of me in formulating a solution. This way, I don't have to do a lot of convincing or selling at the time when action is needed. They are already there and ready to do what it takes.

Change in our rapidly changing world has become a drug, and we are often addicted. We expect change and can become bored if we don't get it. We expect software and apps to be updated every few months. If the features and power of the system are improving, then the change can be beneficial. If the changes only add complexity without adding value, then we must beware. On the other hand, some change comes at us from sources outside of our control, such as government regulations or improving business practices with which we must comply. Often, these kinds of changes can be a complex challenge. The good news is that our competitors have the same challenge, and if we can find a way to comply in a simple, effective manner, we can turn the challenge into a competitive advantage for our company.

The Food Safety Modernization Act (FSMA) is the most radical revamping of food industry standards in over fifty years. The FDA has published about five thousand pages describing the final rules, with more to come. My job was to read all those pages and then distill them down to what really matters. I cannot ask every manager and supervisor in the company to read all that material. That would be a huge waste of time, and we would end up with chaos with different interpretations. My challenge was to condense and interpret the verbiage into a simple and actionable set of steps. This was critical to our ability to manage the change in an efficient manner. Managing change and complexity in a simple, effective, balanced manner is the challenge.

Critical Thinking

Critical thinking is balanced thinking. Achieving balanced thinking requires that we consider all sides of an idea or situation to find the good, the bad, the incomplete, the risky, the right, and the wrong. If we fail to consider all the aspects in a balanced manner, we risk making a decision that will result in failure. Critical does not mean negative, fixed, or closed thinking but rather analytical, flexible, insightful, and open thinking. Critical thinking is needed for problem solving and for assessing the quality of the information that is provided to us.

The ability to think critically is rare in my experience and, like most skills, requires active learning to acquire. I've looked for books and seminars on the subject but find them to be too cookbook to be really useful. Kempner Trego is one of the best programs. It is very prescriptive, and in some cases, the disciplined approach that they apply may be beneficial, especially when it is necessary to push the process beyond what is obvious or already known. Imposing a severely disciplined process helps us avoid what are probably the two biggest errors in the critical-thinking process—namely that we jump from problem to solution without accurately defining the problem and without adequately investigating all the options. The goal of the process is to identify the root cause of the failure we are investigating. If we find the real root cause and eliminate it, we can actually prevent the failure from happening again. If we only identify and address some of the contributing factors, then we can expect the failure to happen again and again. This is where most of us live because we are not thinking in a critical, balanced manner.

It is common to approach problem solving using brainstorming techniques like Fishbone Analysis or 5-Whys Analysis. These are excellent tools but are inadequate substitutes for critical thinking. These techniques will only reveal to us what we or someone else on our team already knows. If we have a brilliant team and they know all the potential root causes and contributing factors, then a disciplined brainstorming technique will uncover it, and we will brilliantly solve the problem. However, since these techniques can only identify what we already know, they are inherently weak techniques. If our team is not aware of the root cause, or it is not obvious, then these techniques will fail. A better option is to collect data and analyze it to identify the real root cause. This is a strong technique that can allow us to go beyond what we already know to identify a root cause of which we are not aware. This is truly brilliant! Collect good data related to the problem and analyze it from many different angles while looking for patterns and trends. Is there any pattern or unusual feature in the data? If so, dig deeper. You may need to collect more data to analyze the unusual feature or pattern you have found. Keep digging by collecting data and asking lots of questions about what you find until you discover what is causing the pattern or unusual feature.

Sometimes, if no one else asks the difficult question, then you need to. A well-placed question can help the team to open up to discuss an uncomfortable issue. Perhaps you made a mistake and no one on the team feels comfortable bringing it up. In the interest of having a complete discussion that considers all aspects of the situation, you need to. Maybe you have information that the team doesn't have, enabling you to see an issue that they haven't considered. There is no better way to show others your leadership ability and to galvanize the team behind you than to be the one who points out the dead cat in the room that we all see (or should see) but all make believe is not there.

Another function of critical thinking is to assess the quality of the information we are receiving. We want to assess in an open and objective manner the information that we are receiving to understand it and to determine if it is accurate or useful. Some questions to ask include the following:

- What is this about?
- Has the problem been defined accurately, completely, and precisely?
- What data was gathered?
- How was it gathered?
- Does the data match the definition of the issue?
- How was the data analyzed?
- What statistics were applied?
- What do the numbers say?
- Do we need to go back to gather more data, or is the data we have sufficient?
- What is missing?
- What could go wrong?
- What conclusions were reached?

Here are the most common failures in critical thinking and investigating to identify the root cause:

- The definition of the problem was incomplete or inaccurate.
- The data collected was incomplete, inaccurate, contains errors, or is not statistically significant.
- We didn't collect any data!

- We used only brainstorming techniques to identify the cause of the issue.
- We confuse a contributing factor with the root cause.
- The corrective actions we take are addressed at correcting the contributing factors, not the root cause.
- The corrective actions we take do not correct or eliminate the root cause.

So, how do we improve our critical-thinking skills? I wish there were an easy or fast way, but I don't know of any. It takes years of focused effort to develop the skill. Here are a few steps that you can take:

- Critical thinking is a process that must be learned and practiced in order to be good at it. Practice! In any situation, ask lots of questions. Consider the implications of what you are hearing or seeing and ask, Does it make sense? If not, then ask questions. Ask, "Where did you get that information? How did you come to that conclusion? How did you collect that data?"
- Critical thinking requires some basic knowledge of a situation that can often only be gained by experience or reading on the subject. Knowledge of the subject is the grist for the critical-thinking mill. If the mill is empty, then there is not much to be done! Immerse yourself in the subject, talk to the people who work there, ask questions, make observations, read anything you can find.
- Critical thinking takes time. In this day of constant distractions, we can find it difficult to find the time to think critically. I find it useful to spend some quiet time every day reflecting on the challenges I am facing. Consider the pros and cons of the actions you have taken and potential next

steps. Try to look at the situation from the perspective of the other people involved. This takes some time and thought, so if you're singing along with the radio, you cannot do it!

Edward de Bono's book *The Six Thinking Hats*[13] is an excellent study on how to enhance the critical-thinking skills of a team. His method is to assign six different-colored hats to the members of a team. Each hat requires the wearer to approach the problem from a different perspective. This assures that the team will consider all aspects of the problem and avoid groupthink. An important critical-thinking skill is to realize that all issues, like coins, have at least two sides. The team needs to consider all sides of the issue— the good, bad, positive, and negative elements. After we think we have found a potential root cause, we need to turn the coin over and consider how we could be wrong. What can go wrong with our analysis and conclusions?

Constructive Criticism

Part of balancing challenge is how we communicate it to our team. Balance is required to assure that they hear the good and the not-so-good feedback. The not-so-good communication may be framed as constructive criticism, an oxymoron if ever there was one. How can criticism be constructive? It almost never is. Our intent in criticizing another person may be that they take the message to heart and use it in a constructive fashion to improve their behavior. That would be a good result. However, the fact is that they almost never accept it in a constructive fashion. People usually deny the criticism and blame us or someone else for what is going wrong. The result is that their behavior does not change, and we now have a wounded person who thinks we are out to get them. Nothing is more dangerous than a wounded person. They will defend themselves any way they can. Their subsequent behavior will likely be defensive and irrational, which could make them difficult to deal with in the future. The downside risk of delivering what we had hoped to be constructive criticism is large.

The old saying that the road to hell is paved with good intentions applies here as well. Our intentions for the other person are good. We really want to help them, and we know how! How can we help without getting into trouble? The best way is to wait until they ask for help. If it looks like hell might freeze over before that happens, the safest way (but not always safe) is to ask a question. Keep it simple, direct, not leading, and not accusatory. Remember you are walking in a minefield.

- "Would you like to talk about the Smith project?"
- "I understand that the Smith project is creating a challenge. Would you like to talk about how we can approach those challenges?"
- "I know you have put a lot of effort into the Smith project. May I discuss some other ideas with you?"

It is tricky, but if the price is worth it, you need to make the attempt. Stay humble and offer your ideas—ideas that they can use or not use as they see fit. You cannot force them to see things your way. See the section on verbal defense. It is a technique of walking with them first to gain rapport and then slowly moving them into a different direction that can be effective. Use questions to get them to consider other ideas. If you can get them to come up with a solution and adopt it as their own, you have succeeded. If they think it is your idea, then you have probably failed. Read Benjamin Franklin's autobiography to see how he was able to convince others to create what are now common institutions—a public library, a community hospital, a city university, a volunteer fire department, and so on. He was instrumental in getting community support for these projects by convincing others that the idea was theirs and not his. His autobiography is a delightful and insightful little book into the life of a very effective and versatile person.

When giving any kind of advice, preface it with a positive statement. For example, instead of "Hey, that tie is not appropriate for the work environment," consider instead, "I appreciate that you wore a tie today to show respect for our visitors; however, may I suggest that a more conservative selection might have been more appropriate." Or if you have a good rapport with the person, maybe making a joke of it can get the point across in a low-anxiety manner: "Where in hell did you get that tie?" or "I'm sure our visitors appreciate that you wore a tie today, but where did you find that one?" See the section on authentic leadership on how to use humor to communicate a tough message. The idea is to get the point across with as little anxiety as possible, unless of course you want to create anxiety. If it is the third or more time you have sent the message in low-anxiety fashion, perhaps it's time to spice it up with some heat.

Swimming with Sharks

A common challenge we will face in leadership is the ability to work with difficult people. We also need to consider that we may be one of those difficult people! The challenge is in how we deal with difficult people. There is a wonderful set of rules originally written by Voltaire Cousteau, who is thought to be a descendent of the philosopher François Voltaire and an ancestor of Jacques Cousteau, about how to swim with sharks. Mr. Cousteau was an expert on sea life, and he wrote the rules as a serious guideline for oyster divers, who were often swimming in the presence of sharks. It is not known when the rules were written, but the author died in 1812. The rules were adapted by Richard Johns for business circumstances and first published for that purpose in 1975 as a *Dinner Address*. The rules are excellent advice for both divers and leaders.

Many leaders are sharks and behave like sharks. They may have risen through the ranks to become the boss due to their aggressive behaviors that turned others into followers or victims. In any case, these people have learned that an aggressive posture works well for them. The rest of us, who have to work with these people, need an effective way to get along and not become a victim. The rules describe what we need to do to achieve that. Sharks, like most bullies, apparently are more bluster than substance in spite of their large size and prominent teeth, and we can make them think twice about attacking us if we don't allow them to intimidate us. I'm not so sure that I'm ready to try the rules with a real shark, but with real people, they work quite well.

RULES FOR SWIMMING WITH SHARKS

1. Assume all unidentified fish are sharks until proven otherwise
2. Don't get cut
3. If you get cut, don't bleed
4. If you get bumped, bump back harder
5. If someone else gets cut, get out of the water

The rules suggest that we can save ourselves from harm by considering that other people may be sharks, and therefore not our friends, until they prove themselves otherwise. We must be careful not to get cut when we are with a shark. Sharks are dangerous and will try to cut us with their sharp words, criticism, or superior attitude. We can avoid getting cut if we don't become defensive by simply and unemotionally stating what we have done and plan to do. Do not defend yourself. When we become defensive, we put ourselves in a weak position that invites further attacks. Defending is admitting that we are wrong or weak. We want to remain strong, rebuffing the attack with statements about our position and what we have done without defending.

If we slip and allow ourselves to get cut by the shark's aggressive behavior, we cannot allow ourselves to bleed. This means that we cannot be weak or show signs of weakness. If we are weak, the shark will attack and finish us off. Our position will be severely compromised, and we may never recover. Sharks love to bump to see how you will react. If you react negatively or defensively, they will keep bumping you until you are cut and your position compromised. They have won. If you bump them back in a professional manner, they will be surprised and not know what to do. They will retreat and reconsider the risk of attacking you. You may not be the easy target that they were expecting. They will have to reassess just how strong you are, and this gives you time to prepare yourself for the next attack if there is one. The best part of bumping back is that the other fish you work with will take notice, and they will also decide that it's not such a good idea to attack you. You will gain their respect as well. Lastly, if someone else gets cut, there is not much you can do to help them if they are not willing or able to help themselves. At best, you may save them today, but since they are weak, they will be open to attack again soon. At worst, you will appear as weak as they are and lose your position of strength. The rules are a simple model based on the behavior of real sharks and real fish, but they can be instructive when applied to the interaction of human sharks and human fish.

Handling Complexity

A skill worth developing in today's harried world is to be able to handle the continuous stream of information that is coming at us relentlessly every minute. This flood of data will distract or confound us if we don't deal with it effectively. Here are some tips on how to maintain your balance.

1. Increase your bandwidth. This takes practice. Challenge yourself to handle more data in a shorter period of time. I make it a game to see how quickly I can scan an email, report, presentation, or even a book to discover the key points, decide on what action I need to take (maybe nothing), and then file it if I may need access to it in the future.

2. Recognize that data is raw and unprocessed with no apparent meaning. Information is data that has been analyzed and organized to have meaning. Data is meaningless and overwhelming. Information is useful and manageable. We need techniques for rapidly converting data into information. Refer to our discussion in chapter 1 about Russell Ackoff's model of mental processing: data, information, knowledge, understanding, and lastly wisdom.

3. Combine the pieces of information into groups. It's easier to manage one hundred pieces of information when the information is organized into five groups than trying to deal with one hundred pieces of distinct information. This is called chunking up. When you can chunk up a bunch of information, you can deal with the information as chunks going forward and not as individual pieces of information. For example, we can try to deal with the Gettysburg Address word by word or chunk it up and deal with it as a single concept. A single chunk can embody

many details that we don't need to carry around—we know what they are and can unpack the chunk any time we need to do so to get at the details. We don't lose the details; we just pack them up inside the chunk and then handle the chunk as a unit going forward. In computer language, we create algorithms or packets of code that we refer to by name, so that we don't have to rewrite the code each time we want to use that algorithm. There is no end to this as we can use algorithms to create new algorithms, to create new algorithms, to create new algorithms, and so forth. The highest-level code is much simpler because we have used and reused existing algorithms without the need to spend time on the complexity embedded in each lower level. We can do the same when we parse data. This data looks like a list of phone numbers—I don't need to read each one; I just need to know that it is a list of phone numbers. If I need an individual phone number in the future, I can come back to this list later and unpack it to find the one that I need. Grouping data into chunks can save a lot of mental energy and time by allowing us to handle complex, high-level information without the need to mentally process all the low-level details that we have neatly put into chunks.

4.   Another form of chunking is processing. We can use an existing process as a chunk. This is called meta processing. If we are working on a design process and want to improve it, we can consider meta design, which is how we design the design process! Of course, this can go on forever too but quickly gets very complicated.

5.   Make lists! As soon as you identify something as a task or discover a piece of useful information, write it down. Once you write it down, you no longer have to exert any mental energy to keep it active. You can forget it, or at least not worry about it, and use your mental energies for processing new data. Worrying

about getting something done has to be the worst waste of mental energy. Don't do it. The important thing is that you have a good filing process and are able to find the information when you need it. Pay attention to how you structure your lists and notes to allow you to quickly find the information you have recorded. Today, searching for a key word can make it possible to find anything; the problem is that there may be so many hits that it is still impossible to find the one that you need. Hierarchical folders are useful to reduce the volume in a search. I practice each time I file something to follow a logical process to determine where it should go. I even have a folder called "I have no idea where to put this!" so that I don't spend a lot of time on the very few pieces of information that have no obvious place to go. Sometimes I scare myself when, years later, I repeat the mental filing process in order to find the information, and it is exactly where I thought it should be!

6. Review your lists often. I have daily and forever lists. Everything big goes into the forever list so that I don't lose these precious ideas and things to do. I go through the forever list periodically to remind myself and to see if there is some step or simple task that I can do to advance any project just a little today. If so, these steps go on my today list. I try to keep my today list reasonable yet challenging. My commitment to myself is to get my today list done today. Sometimes a few slip to tomorrow if I am lazy or if plans change. If you find that you never get your today list done, ask why. Are you putting too much on the list, or are you allowing too many distractions?

7. Watch yourself. If you find yourself saying that you don't have time to do something that is important, this could be a sign of poor planning. A good metaphor for managing our daily list of tasks is a fish tank. If we fill the tank with water (tasks

and distractions), there is no room for adding rocks (important tasks). If we start by adding a few big rocks (critical tasks), then smaller ones (important tasks), and finally the water (small tasks and some distractions), it all fits. When we plan our work for today, put a few big rocks in first. The other thing to watch out for is when we think, *I need two hours to work on this task, and I will not be able to do that, so I cannot work on this today.* If we think this way, we will never do the work, as we may never have two hours free for that alone. Break it up into small pieces and put the small pieces on your today list; get one done this morning, one this afternoon, and so on until in a few days it is done. Don't wait until you have the time. I like to say that we never *have* time, we must *make* time.

8.   Recognize the difference between the important and the urgent. Too often, we allow urgent but not important tasks to crowd out what is truly important but not urgent. The consequence is that the important work never gets done. When I put a task on my forever list, I put a deadline so I know when it has to be done. This doesn't work for tasks that don't have a deadline. We can either create an artificial deadline or take the important task and break it up into small pieces, committing to getting one piece done today. Repeat this until it is done.

9.   Celebrate! When you complete a task, no matter how small, take a second to look back at what you have done and give yourself a mental pat on the back for a job well done. You can give yourself a treat like a cup of coffee or a five-minute break. Rewarding ourselves when we complete a task feels good and can motivate us in the future to get that list taken care of!

10. Time is the one resource that we all get the same amount of. Jeff Bezos doesn't get any more time in a day than we do. The

difference between him and us is how we spend our time. Sleeping less, working harder, socializing less, and eating less are all possible ways to get more time to do what we want to do each day, but there is a price to be paid. It is much better for us to make more effective use of the time we have than to steal precious time from these other essential activities.

You have to apply yourself each day to becoming a little better. By applying yourself to the task of becoming a little better each day over a period of time, you will become a lot better.
—UCLA basketball coach John Wooden

The "New Broom" Speech

When you take over a position, how do you behave and what do you say? How do you address your new team as their new leader so that everyone is clear about your goals? You will want to share your mission, vision, and values in the context of the balance you will strive to achieve as the leader. Too often, a new leader loses this golden opportunity that exists only for a short time at the very beginning of their tenure. You want to take advantage of the opportunity of being seen as the new broom that will come in to sweep clean where the old broom left behind some dirt. You don't want to blame your predecessor but rather point out how you will be different. Sometimes it is clear to everyone that you are here to make a change. Other times, things are going well, so people may expect that you will carry on in the same manner as the previous leader. It is up to you to define the goals with input from your boss and your team. Just because things are going well doesn't mean that we don't need to do better, and it doesn't guarantee that we will continue to do well in a changing world. This is your opportunity to set the balance and agenda for your term as leader of the group. Take it!

Here is an outline of the points that you want to include in your "New Broom" speech:

- a brief outline of your background so people know who you are
- brief introductions of your team members so you know who they are and what they do
- your view of the current performance—being respectful to the past regime
- your view of current challenges to the business—what is changing that could derail us
- your vision of where you want to take the business or group in the next three years
- your goals for how we will all behave to accomplish the vision—setting goals, not expectations
- your values and the values of the group

You can tell a lot from the introductions that your team members give.

- What do they say?
- What don't they say?
- How do they relate to each other?
- Are they working as a team?
- Do they talk to each other, and if so, how?
- Do they joke, or are they deadpan?
- Do they back each other up?

Set team goals and avoid personal expectations that can be perceived as negative or dictatorial. If that is not how you want to lead, then agree on goals and avoid setting expectations. Goals are common to the group and therefore are seen as positive and leading toward the vision. The difference seems subtle but is actually significant. Contrast saying to your team members, "My expectation is that you are on time and prepared for meetings" with "I suggest that we make it a goal to be on time and prepared for meetings."

I prefer a direct approach so that there is less chance of misunderstanding. What I mean is having a discussion with my new team about my vision for the team so that we are aligned. I want their feedback and understanding. It is the first and perhaps most important opportunity for us to come together as a unified team with a common mission, vision, and values. Here is an example of how to approach this conversation.

"Please let me explain how I plan to lead the team. First, I prefer that we discuss and agree on the goals and then work together to achieve them. Second, we will support each other to success. We will not allow anyone to fail, and we will not tolerate failure. Mistakes are inevitable and can be okay as long as we make corrections quickly and don't repeat the mistake. I think it's a good goal to be on time and prepared for meetings, and I encourage you to do so. If any of us discovers a problem, communicate it to the team ASAP. We don't tolerate covering up mistakes. My job is to make each of you successful. That means I will be honest in assessing our performance, including my own. I am not always right, and in many cases, you know your jobs better than I do, so I will rely on you for your feedback and guidance. I invite discussion and will support differing opinions until we make a decision. Then we will all support the decision to success. I will challenge each of you. Our goal is that this business will not be the same in three years, and you and I will also be different in three years. I believe in working hard, being successful, and having fun, in that order! Without hard work, there is no success. Without success, there is no fun. Without fun, there is no hard work. It is a virtuous cycle. Please tell me what your goals are for me and for the team …"

When you are new to a team or company, use the opportunity to set the agenda. Read *The First 90 Days* by Michael D. Watkins[14] for insight into how to do this successfully. You have an opportunity to establish a vision and leadership style with the team that will not come again.

The Future of Challenge

We all need a challenge to define our future. There are three kinds of challenges: challenges that we define for ourselves; those that we allow others to impose or define for us; and those that happen due to uncontrollable or unpredictable events. Henry Kissinger said, "There cannot be a crisis next week. My schedule is already full." We can live minute to minute, dealing in a reactionary manner to the challenges that life and work throw at us. Or we can establish goals to guide our activities in a forward-thinking manner. This is how we make real progress toward a meaningful goal. Reacting to life's challenges may be challenge enough, but this is an aimless journey. We may be satisfied with the results if we are part of a team or company where others are defining a good direction and creating meaningful challenge for us. However, on the other hand, we are allowing others to define the direction, and perhaps after some time we will discover to our dismay that the place we have arrived at is not what we really wanted. It will be better for us and for our team if we participate in an active manner in defining the goal and the challenges to get there. We are more likely to be satisfied with where we find ourselves some day in the future.

Too much challenge will wear us out and ultimately result in burnout and demotivation. Too little challenge will create complacency and boredom. The proper balance of challenge creates motivation and satisfaction. Achieving this sweet spot is of course a challenge in itself. We must know ourselves and what level of challenge is best for us at this particular time in our career and lives. It will likely change, depending on our attitude and status. It will change as we get older as well, but we should beware of becoming complacent and too comfortable. It may be a warning sign if we find ourselves comfortable with our current position or lacking a significant goal to challenge us. Without challenge, we will stop growing. The result is that our skills become dated, and we become obsolete.

There are lots of ways to create new challenges. One of the best is to introduce some new people into the team. They will likely have a different perspective and see issues and opportunities that we may not see. Another is to set an outrageous goal—a BHAG (big, hairy, audacious goal), as described in the classic book *Built to Last: Successful Habits of Visionary Companies* written by Jim Collins and Jerry I. Porras.[15] A BHAG will take us and our team away from the status quo and challenge us to think differently. We may have done well and may be doing well. That may be the perfect time for a BHAG to create motivation to take performance to a new level. It's better for us to create a BHAG rather than allow a competitor to do it to us. When beverage companies created diet versions of their successful products, it looked at first like a bad move. The new product would take market share away from the original and create manufacturing and market complexity. It would decrease profitability initially. What could not be seen at the time of launch was that, in time, consumer preferences would change, and eventually the new product would become a significant part of sales and profit. The conservative approach would have been to avoid fragmenting the market with a new product and continue to support the original product. In the short term, this would have increased overall profitability. In the long term, this approach would have missed creating a significant new product line with tremendous future profitability. And if they didn't launch it, surely their competitors would have. Many companies will set up a separate team as a skunk works project to develop and launch a new product, to avoid defensive activities by the team responsible for the original product line that could kill the new product before it has a chance to grow and realize full potential.

Another way to create challenge is to get away to think without distractions. Bill Gates, when he was CEO of Microsoft, made an annual two-week pilgrimage by himself to an isolated location, where he could be alone to reflect on the past and imagine the needs of the future. Before going away, he would ask his people to send him proposals for projects and new business opportunities. He would spend the two weeks without interruption, reading the briefs, reading some books he brought along, and just thinking about it all. The retreat had the additional benefit of allowing him to rest both mentally and physically from his grueling job at Microsoft. He would return to work refreshed and full of ideas, ready to guide the company for another year and more.

Challenges don't need to be only an annual event. There is great benefit to defining challenges and goals on a yearly or longer time frame, as the longer period invites us to plan bigger. But there is also a need to set challenges for ourselves every day. A great way to do this is when you first wake up each morning, allow some quiet time to consider what needs to be done today. Try not to get too caught up in the problems or failures from yesterday, although these will often motivate today's work. Go through your list of goals and ask, "What can I do today to advance this goal one step?" Perhaps you can send an email asking for some information. Perhaps you can plan a meeting to discuss a part of the goal. Any little thing you can do today to make progress toward the goal will be beneficial. A journey of a thousand miles begins with one step. Take that step today.

Another fun way to create a challenge is to observe where everyone is going and then to go in the opposite direction. Students of rhetoric do this. Each picks a side of the issue, one pro and one con, and then regardless of their personal beliefs, they must develop and deliver a convincing argument. It is good practice and intellectually stimulating, especially supporting a position that you don't agree with. This can help us to avoid herd mentality. The herd may be right and may be going in the right direction, today. However, almost surely, conditions will eventually change, and needs will change. The herd will continue going in the same direction even though it is no longer the right direction. If you have prepared yourself to do the opposite, when conditions change, you can be way ahead of the herd. Another way to do this is to foster contrarian thinking in yourself and your team. Contrary doesn't mean negative or destructive thinking but rather thinking that considers the other side of the coin. It's always good to do this to avoid unpleasant surprises due to unanticipated consequences. Don't be afraid to ask what may appear at the time to be "stupid" questions. Remember: there are no stupid questions, only stupid answers.

Teasing is a fun way to create challenge. Lighthearted teasing and banter can keep the conversation with those around us fresh and cheerful. Teasing is often contrarian by nature and sometimes will spur or reveal a good idea or raise an interesting question that we hadn't considered. And since it is done in a lighthearted manner, there are no hard feelings or bruised egos. A team that can tease and cheerfully challenge each other will perform better, have more fun, and stay together longer.

Doing the same job every day repeatedly can lead to boredom. After repeating a task over and over, we no longer have to think about it. Our thoughts can wander to consider other issues. If the work allows it, perhaps we can be thinking about something else. On one hand, we have to be careful, if we are performing a potentially dangerous job, that we don't allow our minds to wander too far or we could get hurt. We can also make the boring work competitive by making it a game. We can compare our speed and accuracy to our own past performance or benchmark against a colleague or competitor. In this manner, we can keep score and challenge ourselves to find ways to improve speed or accuracy. The result is good for performance and makes the boring job more fun and rewarding for us. One day when John D. Rockefeller was walking around one of his plants, he stopped to watch a worker apply solder to seal a can. He asked the worker how many drops of solder he was applying. The answer was seven. He asked, Could he do it just as well with six drops? The worker had been instructed to use seven and never tried less. He agreed to try and found that six worked just fine. Of course, then Mr. Rockefeller asked if five would work. It was a good day for Mr. Rockefeller, the company, and the worker, all of whom benefitted from a simple challenging question.

Making a challenge relevant and meaningful improves the motivation to achieve it. A 10 percent increase in sales year over year seems to be a logical and typical challenge. However, what does it mean? Every year, we aim for 10 percent, so it becomes a habit. There are many ways to give the goal some meaning to make it more real. Perhaps we need a 10 percent increase in sales revenue to maintain profitability while absorbing the increased costs of overhead, labor, inflation, and taxes. Maybe our plant has 30 percent free capacity, and our goal is to fill up the line within three years to coincide with our capital plan to invest in a new line at that time. Defining the challenge in the context of reality makes it more real and more motivational. We are all more motivated by a challenge that has a tangible result—other than just reaching some arbitrary goal and making our bonus.

Sometimes to find the optimal point or balance, we have to challenge the system. When adding spice to a recipe, for example, if you don't experiment and on one occasion add too much, you will never know if a little more might be even better. The attitude and practice of constant challenge allows us to test the system to see if we really are at the optimal balancing point. Natural stresses in the environment will often do this for us, but why wait for an uncontrolled event? It is much better for us to create the challenge under controlled conditions and watch how the system behaves. When engineers evaluate the earthquake suppression system on a high-rise building, they place motion sensors and then stand on the roof, gently pushing back and forth with their legs. The repeated motion of their bodies is enough of a stress to set the building into motion. The motion sensors record how the buildings suppression system responds, and analysis will indicate if any adjustments are needed. People tell us not to rock the boat, but if we don't intentionally rock it occasionally, how will we know what will happen when a wave hits us?

Love the Challenge!

Most of us love a good challenge. It keeps us fresh and helps us to improve. Toyota uses a five-year plan to set the goals for the next five years. It is a highly publicized event, and everyone in the company participates. The chairman reveals the challenges that will define the goals for the next five years. A few cycles ago, he set the challenge to reduce the labor cost per vehicle by half in the subsequent five years—a challenging and ambitious goal to be sure. A goal that would help put Toyota ahead of the competition. The engineers and operations people went to work, and within the next five years, they achieved the goal through improved efficiency and automation. When the next five-year plan was revealed, the chairman congratulated the company for achieving the goal and then announced that in the next five years, he was challenging them to do it again!

It feels really good to achieve against a real and meaningful challenge. Leadership will have the opportunity to demonstrate their skill and value by helping the people achieve the challenge. Success is the best reward. People are naturally competitive. We all want to be on the winning team. We hate to lose, even in situations where we know that one team must win and one must lose. As Vince Lombardi said, "Winning isn't everything, but losing is nothing." We all want to win.

The world is changing. Our competitors are changing. Maybe our future competitor doesn't even exist yet. Bill Gates once said that the competitor he most feared was a couple of guys in a garage. Anticipating the changes that are coming is a real challenge. But if we have a business or a successful group, we have an advantage. We have skills, resources, and strategic capabilities. How we leverage those to address future challenges will make all the difference. We can use our strengths to leapfrog the competition, even those in the garage, to develop new strategic capabilities and put even more distance and higher barriers between us and our competition. Or we can rest on our success and wait for someone to catch or surpass us. It is much better to control our own destiny by being proactive in challenging ourselves than waiting to react when someone else challenges us.

One of my favorite stories is how Proctor and Gamble was able, via productivity improvements, to absorb all cost increases in Tide detergent for a period of fifteen years. Their biggest customer is Walmart, and for fifteen consecutive years, they did not pass on a cost increase to Walmart. Do you think Walmart loves P&G? How about the competition? Not so much. Are you old enough to remember Wisk detergent? Wisk was the main competitor to Tide back in the eighties. It was made by Unilever, a rather successful company with tremendous resources. Tide outcompeted Wisk to the point that Wisk is now a distant second-tier brand. Unilever sold the brand to Sun Products in 2008, and in 2017, they discontinued it. P&G didn't just compete with Wisk; they destroyed it by offering service and low cost that Unilever couldn't match.

The ability to think critically is difficult to teach and in fact can probably only be learned by focused effort. It is the one skill that most defines successful leaders, especially those who make it to upper management. Watch a top leader at a meeting. They will listen and watch quietly and then ask one question that goes to the core of the issue. They are able to distill and analyze the jargon, hype, and extraneous information to find the root issue and then bring focus to that issue.

The future is coming whether we like it or not. Be prepared and get your teams prepared. A great way to do this is to perform a risk assessment to identify potential risks and situations where loss can occur in an extreme event. There are lots of good books on the classical methods, but I find these to be too cookbook to be really useful. I suggest reading *The Risk Management of Everything, Rethinking the Politics of Uncertainty* by Michael Power (2004).[16] Then please read my chapter on risk management in *Juran's Quality Handbook*, seventh edition (2016).[17] A good risk assessment can be highly educational for the team and help to build awareness of potential risks. We cannot take effective steps to minimize, manage, or eliminate a potential risk until we have made people aware that the risk exists. Effective risk management requires that we balance the cost of preparation and prevention with the risk of loss.

As Abraham Lincoln said, "The best thing about the future is that it comes one day at a time." Challenging ourselves and our teams every day to improve and prepare for the future that is coming will assure our success in that future.

Chapter 6

Making Balanced Decisions

If you think about it, balanced leadership is all about making decisions. Napoleon recognized this when he said, "Nothing is more difficult, and therefore more precious, than to be able to decide." We've already talked about how not making a decision is actually making a decision. We cannot not decide. It is critical to make decisions consistent with our mission, vision, and values. We've talked about the fact that we are often making decisions with incomplete information. In fact, we will almost never have perfect or complete information. There is an inevitable trade-off between the accuracy and completeness of the information we have, versus how long we wait to collect or confirm the information. There is also a trade-off between the value of a decision and how long we can afford to wait to make it. The more valuable a decision, the longer we may want to wait to make sure that the information we have is as complete and accurate as possible. However, the longer we wait, the greater the risk that the decision will be made for us. Someone else or something else may force the issue, and we could lose the opportunity to decide. How we balance these trade-offs will be critical to the outcome and whether we are able to decide and lead effectively.

> One of the most difficult things in life can be
> trying to put all of these things together.
> —Humpty Dumpty

Difficult Decisions

When making difficult decisions, it is useful to consider the risks involved and to take reasonable steps to manage them. Risk management involves assessing the severity and the likelihood that a particular event will happen. If the severity is high, then you need to be prepared. The likelihood of a tornado hitting your building is low even if you live in Kansas, but the severity is high, so it is prudent to take steps to be prepared. If the severity is low, then it may only be worth spending resources if the likelihood is high. Murphy's Law is "If something can go wrong, it will." A corollary of this law is that "Only when nothing can go wrong will everything go right." An engineer friend of mine had a poster hanging in his office that said, "Murphy was an optimist!" I thought this was a hilarious but meaningful statement. Murphy's Law according to a pessimist is "Even when it appears that nothing can go wrong, it still can and will go wrong." All decisions involve risks that we must assess and decide how or if to prepare for. However, often the riskiest decision of all is not to decide, as we lose control of our fate.

We've talked about the importance of having a plan B just in case plan A doesn't work out. We also talked about the need to consider what can change or go wrong. "Expect the best, plan for the worst, and prepare to be surprised," as Dennis Waitley said, is good advice. When making a decision, I always ask, "What is the worst that can happen?" If the worst is not so bad or I am prepared to deal with it, then I feel more comfortable proceeding.

Yogi Berra said, "When you get to the fork in the road, take it." This looks like a trivial way of saying pick a direction and go. Especially when making emotionally charged decisions that impact the lives of many people, it can be difficult to choose which fork to take. It may matter greatly which fork we take—to us, to other people, and to all our futures. If the difficult decision we make is consistent with our mission, vision, and values, we will be more likely to be okay, even if the unexpected happens. We can feel good about the decision and move on. The point is when you get to a fork in the road, you *must* take it—one way or the other—or you are stopped. The world does not stop; it keeps moving with us or without us. Our competition keeps moving too. Money continues to be spent or made. We must make a choice and move on. It matters deeply which way we go, but go we must.

Sometimes it helps when making a difficult decision to change your physical perspective. Stand in a different part of the office. Move to a different chair. Take a walk. Talk to a friend. Go somewhere quiet and talk to yourself. Consider how other people will view the decision. The different location and change in perspective can help you to see other sides of the issue and perhaps help in making a better decision. Another technique I like to use in decision making is to consider how I might look upon this decision and the potential outcomes when I am ninety years old and looking back over my life.

- Is there the potential that I might regret this decision?
- Did I play it safe and miss the opportunity when it was presented?

- Did I do well when I could have done great?
- Did I compromise on my values or shortchange my goals in the decision?

The last thing I want to do when I am ninety is to look back and have a regret that I could have done better.

> No problem can be solved with the same
> consciousness that created it.
> —Albert Einstein

Are there *good* decisions and *bad* decisions? Can a decision ever be said to have been a mistake? We judge decisions by the consequences that follow. I suggest to you that there are no good or bad decisions. There are good or bad consequences to our decisions. The question is whether we are satisfied with or willing to live with the consequences of our decisions. It's often difficult to predict accurately the potential consequences of a decision at the moment we are making it. However, that is what we must do. First, have we considered all the options? We are often in a rush to make the decision—perhaps with no good reason other than to get it over with and move on to something else. The urgency depends on the circumstances, of course. Take as much time as you reasonably can to identify the options and get help from your staff and outside resources. There are probably a lot more options available than are immediately apparent, and a team with time can do a good job of identifying them. Then, consider the potential consequences. We can get into trouble when we fail to identify the potential consequences. We can make what appears to be a good decision, but if we overlooked a negative consequence, that good decision can turn into a very bad decision. This is called a revenge effect. No decision is ever completely free of bad consequences. And no decision is completely free of good consequences. This is often the root of major disagreements between people. I think you made a terrible decision because I am focused on a negative consequence of the decision that you are not concerned with. You think you made a great decision because you based your decision on a positive consequence that I am not interested in. No wonder we cannot agree.

An example of a bad decision with a good consequence is the discovery of mustard gas as an effective chemotherapy drug. Mustard gas was used as a weapon in WWI and was released in an accident during WWII, resulting in many deaths. Doctors assigned to study the effects of the poisonous gas noticed that it had selectively killed fast-growing cells in the body. They reasoned that it could be used to treat cancer. Tests proved them right, and the first and one of the most effective chemotherapy drugs was discovered. It was a bad decision to use mustard gas as a weapon of war, with a good, unanticipated consequence.

> What glory would attend the discovery, if I could
> banish disease from the human frame, and render
> man invulnerable to any but a violent death!
> —Victor Frankenstein (from the book
> *Frankenstein* by Mary Shelley)

Where does intuition fit into decision making? Is it appropriate to consider intuition when making a decision? These are difficult questions. We all have felt (and feel is the right word) that a decision we are about to make is wrong. We may have no facts or reasons to support this feeling; we have gathered the facts and gone through the appropriate steps to arrive at what appears to be a good decision that we can justify, but it just doesn't feel right. That can be disturbing because we don't know why it feels bad when it looks so good. We are concerned that we are making a mistake in spite of all the good evidence to the contrary. Listen to your intuition and then decide. If you have difficulty making decisions, perhaps your intuition is part of the problem. There is good scientific evidence that your brain is able to assimilate facts and observations that you may not be aware of. On the other hand, your intuitive feelings could be derailing your cognitive brain and causing indecision. Read the book *Blink, The Power of Thinking without Thinking* by Malcolm Gladwell[18] to learn more about how to accept your intuition in the decision-making process. I suggest that you listen to your intuition and fit your feelings into your overall decision-making process, but of course do not make decisions only based on your intuition.

It is by logic that we prove, but by intuition that we discover.
—Henry Poincare

Developing a Strategy

Most people have a difficult time differentiating strategy from goals. There is a hierarchy to high-level planning that starts at the top with a vision, then a strategy to achieve the vision, then goals, and finally tactics or actions. The balance is in developing a strategy that adequately describes how we will achieve the vision by directing our goals. Here are some more detailed definitions.

Vision—a description of a future state that we want to achieve. It is not a dream, because it is feasible. We may never completely get to the desired state, as it may describe an aspirational condition, but it is real and meaningful enough to unite us and drive our behavior. Visions can last and not change for years or even forever. The vision answers the question, What do we want to be or achieve? An example: to be a low-cost producer.

Strategy—a high-level description of how we will approach our vision. It is the manner or way in which we approach the work. Strategies are somewhat more flexible than visions and can flex as conditions change, but good strategies often endure for many years and sometimes forever, driving the development of capabilities that are unique and foundational to our organization. The strategy answers the question, How will we achieve the vision? For example, to achieve our vision to be a low-cost producer, our strategy could be to develop world-class processes in automation and process control.

Goals—a concrete and achievable result. The goal describes success. It must be definite and sufficiently detailed so there is no misunderstanding of what we want to accomplish. Goals define what, who, and when and are used to hold ourselves accountable. The balance between leading and managing is tipping toward managing as we define and accomplish goals. The object of a goal is to break up what needs to be done to achieve the strategy into bite-sized pieces. These pieces or projects can take a day to accomplish or three years, depending on the scope and complexity. It is usually best to break big goals up into smaller ones to drive the work and keep us on track. We don't want to wait three years to find out that we have drifted and will not reach the goal. Breaking it up into small pieces makes the work easier to execute and ensures that we stay on track. The goal answers the question, What is the result we want to accomplish? Goals are defined and changed as needed, usually annually but possibly longer for complicated goals or much shorter for more focused goals. For example: to support our strategy to develop world-class processes in automation, a first goal might be to benchmark and define what it means to be world-class in automation, by identifying the key industry players and owners of the expertise and ways in which we can gain access to the technology. That is a real, actionable, and necessary step to achieve our strategy.

Tactics—the actions or work we do to achieve a goal. Even a goal that takes one day to reach may be comprised of several steps. Tactics change as needed and when needed, depending on our progress toward the goal and on conditions around us. As the world changes, our tactics need to adjust. The tactics answer the question, What will we do? For example, to achieve our goal of benchmarking and defining world-class automation, our action step today could be to perform a literature search for cutting-edge automation providers.

We sometimes confuse strategic projects with strategy. The strategy is the strategy. A strategic project is still just a project or a goal. Calling a project "strategic" doesn't make it strategic. Every project we work on should be a "strategic project" in that all work should be driven and guided by the strategy. Any work or project that is not aligned with the strategy should not be performed. Calling a project a "strategic project" is an oxymoron or a warning flag that someone is trying to force me to work on something that is important to them but maybe not so important or strategic to me or my business.

An easy way to think about strategy is to consider our strategic capabilities. As a person or as a business, we need to have, develop, and maintain certain strategic capabilities that enable us to achieve our vision. These strategic capabilities often define us or our business. These capabilities differentiate us from our competitors and can be a powerful barrier to entry that enables us to maintain a superior position or market share. It can be instructional for us to identify these strategic capabilities—the ones we already possess and the ones we need to develop. Then we can identify goals and tactics to maintain the strategic capabilities we have and to develop the ones we will need in the future. Developing strategic capabilities is long-term work that can take decades to accomplish. Achieving the strategic capability is a game changer for our business and therefore the reason why it is strategic.

Here are some examples of business strategic capabilities:

1. Innovation
2. People development and retention
3. Product delivery system

4. Density of products delivered to the market
5. Brand (well known and trusted)
6. Manufacturing low cost (volume, complexity, technologies, automation)
7. Product quality (equal to or better than competition)
8. Price on the retail shelf (proportional to the value delivered)
9. Systems (integrated, effective, efficient, up-to-date systems that support the operations and distribution)
10. Supply chain that is efficient (minimal carrying cost), flexible, responsive, capable (quality), safe, and innovative

It takes decades of focused and persistent hard work to develop strategic capabilities such as these. Once you have developed them, it takes more hard work and diligence to maintain or enhance them. Possessing strategic capabilities such as these makes it difficult for a competitor to challenge your business. It will take them years to replicate what you have done, and by the time they accomplish it, you will have developed your capabilities that much further, preventing them from catching up. These capabilities work together to create an integrated and supporting business climate that is difficult to replicate or displace. These are all reasons why these capabilities are strategic.

Ignorance, Negligence, and Diligence

We need a foundation for making decisions. The best foundation is to follow Russell Ackoff's model for thought processing in reverse. Wisdom is better than understanding, understanding is better than knowledge, knowledge is better than information, and information is better than data. As leaders, we need to assess what we know when making a balanced decision.

Ignorance may be bliss in some circumstances—but not in business. Telling the police officer who pulls you over to advise you that he clocked you at fifty miles an hour that you didn't know the speed limit was twenty-five is not an effective defense. Ignorance is not an adequate defense when it comes to regulations or good business practices. You must be aware and keep yourself up to date. Join trade groups that are active in your industry. They are a great source of information and make it their job to keep up on the latest regulations and practices. You cannot afford to be ignorant.

Negligence is failing to take action when you are aware and able to do so. In many countries, negligence is a civil crime when it results in loss or harm to another person. When you learn that you or someone in your company has made a mistake, you now have information and are required to act. When a decision must be made, you must be active in making it happen. Indecision or inaction can be negligence. You need to assess the situation, identify your options, and then take appropriate action in a reasonable amount of time. That is diligence. Perhaps you or others in your company made a decision and took action that has had an unexpected negative consequence. As soon as you recognize the undesired or unanticipated negative consequence of your action, you must act diligently and quickly or risk being negligent. You can plead ignorance, but that is a weak and inexcusable defense.

Diligence is the position we want to be in when making important decisions. We have taken active steps to educate ourselves about the situation and then taken feasible steps to minimize or eliminate the potential risks. The result is a decision that anticipates the potential failures and allows action in order to assure a favorable outcome.

Fight or Flight!

We will encounter difficult, complicated, uncertain, and messy situations. How we manage these situations, if we choose to manage them, will define us as leaders and people. Avoiding conflict can be a wise decision. On the other hand, it may be important for us to take a stand or at least explain how we are thinking about the situation. A good option can be to ask everyone to step back and review the vision, mission, values, strategy, and goals. This review may help remind everyone what we want to achieve and how we want to behave. This can clear the air and expose any activities that are not balanced or aligned. Then perhaps we can lead the team to a better decision without conflict.

A useful model when considering how to balance our behavior is to consider that we are composed of four parts: head, hands, heart, and feet.

- We use our feet to take us toward, or to run away from, a problem.
- We use our head to think, solve problems, and improve.
- We use our hands to get the work done.
- We use our heart to care to do what is right, even when it is difficult.

Too often, we leave our minds and hearts at home. We come to work to use our hands as we have been taught. We run away from problems, as this can lead to conflict or more work. Engaging people's hearts and minds in the work is a result of effective leadership. We cannot force people to care or think. These are voluntary behaviors that people must offer freely because they want to. Remember that we cannot effectively motivate people; we can only influence them and support them to want to care and think. The leader does this by caring and thinking. When contemplating a difficult situation, it can be useful and instructive to think out loud in front of your people. By doing this, you can accomplish several important results. You can show them that you are human and not so sure what to do either. You can help them see how you approach a difficult situation. You can show them how you go back to our vision, mission, values, strategy, and goals as you contemplate the situation. You can show them how you identify options and then evaluate each according to our vision, mission, values, strategy, and goals to develop and select an option that balances the costs and benefits and will work well. It's a good way to turn a potentially unpleasant situation into a team-building exercise, and when you've reached a conclusion, you have also developed alignment and understanding in your team.

Please notice that the mouth is not mentioned as one of the parts. This is because what we say is not so important. What matters most is what we do. Too often, the mouth becomes the most used part of a leader. The ears should be far more important and more used than the mouth. I suggest that the ears should have done their job before we get to the point of contemplating fight or flight. If we haven't listened, then we are not in a position to contemplate or make a decision. The ears are not mentioned in this model, not because they are unimportant but rather because their job must largely be done before we get to this point.

We want our people to engage their hearts and minds while aligning their feet in the right direction so that their hands can get to work and solve the problem!

Judgment

As a leader, you will be called upon often to exercise judgment when making decisions. Good judgment is the process of balancing the pros and the cons of the situation, assessing the consequences, both intended and unintended, considering the mission, vision, and values, considering common sense, considering the potential impact on all parties, and much more. Wisdom and balance are key criteria in good judgments and in making decisions. There is often no clear right or wrong answer, so sometimes you must choose the least offensive option or the least costly. Other times, there will be an overarching element that defines the situation, and all other issues, costs, and consequences become inconsequential. In a business situation, you must often do what is right for the business. This may not be what is best for some people on the team. On the other hand, if one of your core values is to do what is right for the people on your team, in the belief that long term that is what is right for the business, then you may decide differently. Not all decisions require judgment, such as simple choices, but any decision involving trade-offs between multiple issues or when information is incomplete likely will.

Decisions that require judgment are usually important or complicated ones, requiring care and thought. Take your time to consider the options and potential consequences. Talk it over with other people. Look at it from different angles to see if the answer changes. Sleeping on it may help. Your unconscious mind can work on a problem for days with little or no prompting from you. The answer then comes more easily the next time you consider the issue. Give yourself time to contemplate. In our ever-busy world, we don't get enough time to think without interruption. Do you ever have a few minutes where there is no TV, cell phone, email, internet, radio, or other distraction? Find some time when your brain can be quiet. Meditation can be great, but at least give your brain a chance to be quiet for a few minutes so you can think.

Decisions requiring judgment cannot be made in a vacuum. You need perspective that can only come from knowing the situation, based on more than just the facts. Facts are useful but are only a small part of the judgment process. Knowledge, understanding, and wisdom are better. Feelings and intuition can also be useful, helping us to *feel* parts of the problem that are ill defined. Getting help from other people, especially those with experience, can improve the decisions that we make. I always try to bounce my important decisions off of somebody else to get their perspective. Sometimes, just the act of explaining your decision to someone else can expose weaknesses. The quality of our judgment process defines the decisions we make and are capable of making.

An element of judgment that is often overlooked and underappreciated is common sense. It's a sad but true joke to say that common sense is not so common. Common sense is simply asking what makes sense in a situation. What is the right thing to do? If the decision weren't confounded by inconsistent or contradictory facts, a heap of emotion and individuals' passionate commitment to their points of view, what would be the right decision to make for the business? In order to make a good judgment, you may need to divorce yourself from the personal interests of all parties, including your own. What makes sense and what will work?

Making decisions during a crisis can be especially stressful. Good decisions need to be made quickly, often with incomplete or even wrong information. I create crisis teams, and we prepare by practicing against plausible, made-up scenarios. This way, team members get to know their role and what is expected of them. It gives me a chance to assess their ability and provide coaching in a low-risk situation. I take the input from the team and try to assemble it as a story. When pieces fit, it gives us some confidence that we got it right. When pieces don't fit, it tells us that we are missing something or have some wrong information. I ask lots of questions. If there are no answers, we go back to gathering information until we have a logical and reasonably good explanation of what happened. Then we are ready to make a decision about what to do.

> Judgment comes from experience, and
> experience from bad judgment.
> —Simon Bolivar

Justice

Every action has an equal and opposite reaction. This is Newton's third law of motion, and it is just as true in interpersonal relations as it is in physics. Balance in nature. Balance in how we interact with other people. If I hit you, you will hit me back—eventually, and I don't necessarily mean physical hitting (no physics involved!). Likewise, if I do you a favor, you are likely to return the favor—eventually. A difference between people and physics is that the reaction is often stronger than the original action. The person on the receiving end of the action may not react to the first or even second action. The result is that several actions are combined, and when they finally do react, the reaction may be much stronger than the action that precipitated it. Don't be surprised if a seemingly small action on your part results in a strong reaction on someone else's part. My mentor Dr. Charlie Stewart compares this to collecting Green Stamps OR S&H Green Stamps. Supermarkets back in the sixties had a program where you got stamps every time you made a purchase. You put the stamps in a book, and when the book was full, you could redeem it for a gift like a toaster. It's the same concept; we put a stamp in the book every time we get a good or bad feeling from another person, and when the book is full, we redeem it!

There are almost always consequences to our actions. It may take years for the reaction to take place, but it will happen when the moment is right in the other person's mind. If I make someone the butt of a joke, they may absorb the offense and say nothing, but be sure that the score is stored in their memory, to be settled at some time in the future. If I have a string of good luck and things are going well for me, be sure that some observer is feeling a bit jealous and will save that nugget, waiting for the day when they can help serve me what in their mind is justice. Like the Grateful Dead say, "When life looks like easy street, there is trouble at your door." This is not pessimism but rather realism.

The lesson from this rather dour outlook is to be careful when doling out negative comments. There is a price to be paid for them. Also, be careful not to gloat or be too proud when things go well; there is a price to be paid for that too. Work on being positive and appreciative of others. This behavior pays off, and just like money in the bank, the interest compounds!

> The stupid neither forgive nor forget, the naïve forgive
> and forget, the wise forgive but do not forget.
> —Thomas Szasz

We love to see justice done to others. When a "bad" person gets his or her deserved punishment, we feel vindicated. We also feel good when a deserving person gets the reward for which they have worked so hard. We can get into trouble, however, when we feel like we are the judge, jury, and executioner. It is usually not our job or place to dole out justice, no matter how good it feels. Our actions will not be rewarded or looked upon kindly by management if we are creating strife, tension, divisiveness, or just generally behaving badly in order to give someone what we think is their due justice. It is better in most cases to walk away from the scene and allow justice to come at its own pace. One of my favorite sayings is "every dog has its day." I just have to keep doing my job and have enough patience to wait for that day to come!

A difficult lesson for some of us to learn is that justice is simply not your job. You don't have the time or know the situation well enough to be an effective judge. You can hold people accountable to the rules and policy, but focus on performance, not behavior. Assess results, not intentions.

Deciding in Balance

What makes a good decision good? The result of course is what matters. A balanced decision results in a balance of consequences, mostly good; however, we can almost never make a decision that results in only good results. There will always be some negative consequences to the best of decisions. There will always be someone who will not be satisfied with any decision. So, what is the proper balance? That will depend on our values. If a vaccine prevents 9,999 people from getting the flu and from suffering the consequences but results in one person in ten thousand getting the flu, is that an acceptable balance? What if one person in one million gets the flu and dies from it? That unlucky individual may never have contracted the flu and therefore may have lived if they had not taken the vaccine. Situations like this are very difficult or even impossible to assess objectively. There is risk in all human activities, and we must accept the negative consequences in order to enjoy the benefits. The balance in deciding if a decision is good or bad can be very difficult and not precise or definite. There is no good answer or method, except to be as aware as possible of the consequences, both good and bad, the trade-off of cost to benefit, in order to allow for the best judgment and balance possible.

> He who made kittens put snakes in the grass.
> —Jethro Tull

Is there such a thing as an optimal decision? For any given set of circumstances, in theory, there is an optimal decision that best balances the risks, costs, and the benefits. We probably don't have all the information that is necessary, because gathering the data needed would take too long and cost too much. And even if we were able, changes in circumstances would quickly make the optimal decision no longer optimal. The target is moving, and the trade-offs are changing. Making *good* decisions should be our goal, not optimal ones. This all underscores the difficulty of making good decisions but also the value of having leaders who are capable of making good decisions in the absence of complete information. Making good decisions is often more dependent on experience and speed than science and rigor.

Leaders must make hundreds of decisions daily. Steve Wynn describes his role as CEO as the decision maker of last resort. He empowers his people to make any decision they are confident enough to make. When they don't know what decision to make, it ends up on his desk. Then he must make the tough choice, often to pick the less offensive of the options. In a case like this, there are significant potential negative consequences to any decision, including making no decision. This is when a CEO makes their money. They must be aware of the potential negative consequences and be willing and able to manage them when they occur.

Be always sure you are right, then go ahead.
—Davy Crockett (frontiersman and early US congressman)

It's useful for us to keep in mind that our decisions will impact other people—and again, not all good, regardless of our intentions. If there is a potential negative consequence, it may be good to make the parties who will have to bear or manage this consequence aware up front. If they understand the benefits that drive the decision and the potential negative consequences that could impact them or their operation, perhaps they can prepare or compensate. Getting their buy-in up front will minimize the impact of the negative consequences. Dwight Eisenhower said, "A leader is someone who gets other people to do what he wants because they want to." I would paraphrase this as "A leader is someone who gets people to buy into and support a decision that may not benefit them but benefits the greater good."

Social media makes it even faster and easier to criticize a decision, sometimes with tremendous reach and speed. A lot can go wrong in the communication process that follows your announcement. Facts can be left out without consideration of the whole picture, making balance impossible. Unsubstantiated conclusions can be reached and shared with no opportunity for you to explain or respond. The speed with which the discussion spreads makes it impossible to respond effectively. A negative and wrong statement will remain on the internet forever, without any real possibility of removing it, and it can even come back every few months or years, long after it has been debunked. For all of these reasons, effective social media communication is becoming more important every day. When a controversial or potentially impactful decision is made, it is imperative that it be communicated in a clear and concise manner that is difficult to misinterpret or reduce to incomprehension via sound bites. There is no balance in positive communication—more is always better. More communication doesn't necessarily mean more quantity but rather more quality. If your initial explanatory communication failed or was sound-bitten to death, there is not a lot you can do to recover. Any attempt to defend a failed communication will be seen as a cover-up, and your credibility decreases further. If you have credibility, your loyal supporters will speak up on your behalf while you quietly wait for the media attention to fade away, which it usually will, if you have the discipline to keep quiet.

A leader will be judged based on the consequences of their

decisions. Making good decisions is difficult and involves good judgment based on experience, intuition, listening, and learning. Good leaders ask lots of questions, are masters of observation, and use what they hear and see to learn and improve their decisions. They involve others, including the people impacted by a decision, in the process to identify options and assess and select a decision. They make decisions and don't shy away from making the tough but important decisions in a timely manner. They make decisions based on their mission, vision, values, strategy, and goals and keep these in the forefront at all times. They understand that there are good and bad consequences to every decision, they balance the cost with the benefits, and they attempt to minimize the unintended negative consequences. They get consensus on decisions even from those who will be impacted negatively by the decision. They care and think openly and engage their people to do the same. They support their people to success, with the result that their people will accept the tough decisions and walk through walls if necessary, because they feel comfortable and confident that they can. They own the consequences of their decisions and deal with them in a constructive and nondefensive manner. Good leaders are expert at making, communicating, and executing balanced decisions.

Chapter 7

The Final Word—Balance

We've explored the implications of balance in leadership from many perspectives: in leading yourself, in leading others, in communicating, in creating effective challenge, and lastly in making balanced decisions. Finding and dynamically adjusting the decision points to maintain balance is difficult and exciting. The balance you strike defines you as a leader and as a person. You cannot escape it—nor do you want to. Accept the challenge and the fact that you will never achieve perfect or lasting balance. The best way to navigate the constant changes that require you to adjust is like sailing a sailboat or riding a bicycle—constant attention to the current state of balance and anticipation of the need to adjust quickly and effectively. The adjustments must be timely; adjusting too soon or too late will result in losing balance and failing. Transparency and authenticity are your best friends.

Let's finish with a few final summary points on balance in leadership:

- Maintain balance in all things, including balance. Even balance can be overdone.
- The decisions you make and the actions you take or don't take will define you as a person and as a leader.
- Develop a mission, vision, and values, and live by them.
- Keep your mission, vision, and values in mind at all times.
- Communicate your mission, vision, and values in all you say and especially in all that you do.
- Consider the inevitable trade-offs between benefits and costs. Then act with confidence, secure in knowing that you are in balance.
- Develop strategy and goals based on your vision, mission, and values.
- Balance is dynamic, so keep a watch out for evidence that you are no longer in balance.
- Listen to everyone.
- Carefully listen to the stray person who disagrees. They might be right.
- Likewise, consider what the crowd would have you do, but don't necessarily do it! Groupthink is pervasive and dangerous.
- Do what you know is right, and be prepared to live with the consequences.
- When attacked, don't defend; explain what you have done and why. Keep it brief, to the point, and on point.
- Challenge yourself and your people to do better every day.
- Keep learning and make learning an element of everything you do.
- Support your people to success.

A Recipe for Successful Leadership

I am a baker, so I work a lot with recipes and procedures. Baking requires exact measurement and meticulous technique in order to get good and consistent results, but there are as many recipes as there are bakers and grandmas. Just for fun, here is a recipe for successful leadership. I offer this as a way of emphasizing that there is no single recipe for successful leadership, just as there is no single way to lead effectively. There are many ways—as many ways as there are people. Just like baking a cake, there are many ways to be a successful, balanced leader.

Recipe for Successful, Balanced Leadership

One	Whole Mission that describes why your organization exists (what are you here for?)
One	Ripe and well-developed Vision of a future aspirational state for your group (or yourself)
One	Strategy for how we will achieve the vision and make it real
A Handful	Goals to deliver real results according to the strategy (ownership, accountability)
As needed	Tactics (actions) to achieve the goals (what, who, when)
To taste	Add expectations about the results we want to see (feedback)
Liberally	Support the team to success (do not accept or permit failure from anyone)
Three	Key Performance Indicators for each function to allow us to track progress
A pinch	Critical thinking and feedback when results are less than desired (fix it)
A Gallon	Ownership of the results by team members (engagement)
Garnish	With sincere caring about each team member
A bunch	Celebrate and congratulate the team when we succeed
Repeat	Often!

Balance is a wonderful and useful concept to help us be better leaders, as long as we keep balance itself in perspective. Balance, as we have said, is a dynamic and ever-changing point on a continuum from one extreme behavior to another. Finding the sweet spot of perfection will be short-lived and fleeting at best. We will often find ourselves out of balance. We can ignore it—bad. We can deny it—worse. We can try to hide it—disaster! Or we can admit it. "Yep, that idiot out in left field is me! But I did it for a good reason—honest!" Let's allow better judgment to triumph, and we can adjust as necessary. Don't ever expect to get the balance perfect, or at least not for very long. This is what makes leadership such a complex, messy, and ultimately rewarding experience. Learn from the failures, celebrate the successes, and have some fun along the way. Now, that's pragmatic, balanced leadership![19]

Work hard, be successful, and have fun—
in that order and in balance!

Endnotes

1   Bill George and Warren G. Bennis, *Authentic Leadership: Rediscovering the Secrets to Creating Lasting Value* (Hoboken, NJ: Wiley Publishers, 2004).

2   Robert K. Greenleaf, *Servant Leadership* (Mahwah, NJ: Paulist Press, 2002).

3   Larry Bossidy and Ram Charan, *Execution: The Discipline of Getting Things Done* (New York: Crown Business Publishing, 2002).

4   Laurie Beth Jones, *Jesus, CEO: Using Ancient Wisdom for Visionary Leadership* (New York: MJF Books, 1995).

5   Andrew Grove, *Only the Paranoid Survive: How to Exploit the Crisis Points That Challenge Every Company* (New York: Currency Doubleday Publishers, 1996).

6   Russel L. Ackoff, *Ackoff's Best* (New York: John Wiley and Sons, Inc., 1999).

7   Rudolf W. Giuliani, *Leadership* (Collingdale, PA: DIANE Publishing Company, 2005).

8   Alfie Kohn, *Punished by Rewards: The Trouble with Gold Stars, Incentive Plans, A's, Praise, and Other Bribes* (Boston: Houghton Mifflin Harcourt, 1995).

9   Malcolm Gladwell, *The Tipping Point: How Little Things Can Make a Big Difference* (New York: Little, Brown and Company, 2000).

10 John Gray, *Men Are from Mars: Women Are from Venus: A Practical Guide for Improving Communication and Getting What You Want in Your Relationships* (New York: HarperCollins Publishers, 1993).

11 Stuart Brown, MD, *Play: How It Shapes the Brain, Opens the Imagination, and Invigorates the Soul* (New York: Penguin Group, 2010).

[12] Michael Hammer and James Champy, *Reengineering the Corporation: A Manifesto for Business Revolution* (New York: HarperBusiness Publishers, 1993).

[13] Edward De Bono, *Six Thinking Hats* (New York: Little, Brown and Company, 1985).

[14] Michael D. Watkins, *The First 90 Days* (Boston: Harvard Business Review Press, 2013).

[15] Jim Collins and Jerry I. Porras, *Built to Last: Successful Habits of Visionary Companies* (New York: HarperCollins Publishers, 1994).

[16] Michael Power, *The Risk Management of Everything: Rethinking the Politics of Uncertainty* (London: Demos, 2004).

[17] Joseph A. De Feo, *Juran's Quality Handbook, The Complete Guide to Performance Excellence, Seventh Edition* (New York: McGraw Hill Education Books, 2017).

[18] Malcolm Gladwell, *Blink, The Power of Thinking without Thinking* (New York: Little, Brown and Company, 2007).

Index

K

Keith, Kent M., 133
Kempner Trego, 180
Kennedy, John F., 8
key performance indicators
(KPIs), 121
Keynes, John Maynard, 119
King, Martin Luther, Jr., 8–9, 39
Kissinger, Henry, 196
Klem, Bill, 165
Kohn, Alfie, 114

L

Lao Tzu, 35, 36, 86
leadership
authentic leadership, 4–7
being a great leader, 46
as everyone's job, 4
as having many elements, 3
leading versus managing,
22–26, 24t
leading with a vision, 7–15
versus "pushership," 15–22, 16t
recipe for successful leadership,
227–228
strength as critical attribute of,
28–36, 30t
Leadership (Giuliani), 110
leading others
accountability, 119–122
balance in, 102–142
destructive doubt versus power
of dare, 111–112
developing others, 102–107
difficult people, 126–133
fun at work, 137–140
ideas, 116–119

men and women in groups,
136–137
motivation and expectations,
107–111
ownership, 114–116
paying attention, 121–126
rewards and recognition,
112–114
trust, 133–136
leading yourself
adequacy and inadequacy,
70–72
asking questions, 72–74
balance in, 48–101
emotional intelligence, 55–61
learning, 74–81
optimism, 86–88
persistence, 81–86
risking your job to save it,
67–70
smart and wise, 62–66
work-life balance, 88–97
your mission, vision, and
values, 48–55
learning
levels of human mental
processing that result
in, 79t
as part of leading yourself,
74–81
ways of, 80–81
Lincoln, Abraham, 76–77, 144,
160, 204
Ling, Nicholas, 77
listening, talking and, 154–158
lists, use of, 42, 190–191
Lombardi, Vince, 40, 202
Lovell, James, 42
Low, Gary, 55